Our War with SATAN

An Expose of the Devil and His Followers

DR. LAUREN J. BALL

ISBN 978-1-954345-09-6 (paperback)

Copyright © 2020 by Dr. Lauren J. Ball

All rights reserved. No part of this publication may be reproduced, distributed, or transmitted in any form or by any means, including photocopying, recording, or other electronic or mechanical methods without the prior written permission of the publisher. For permission requests, solicit the publisher via the address below.

Rushmore Press LLC
1 800 460 9188
www.rushmorepress.com

Printed in the United States of America

Introduction

There are two absolutes that will happen regardless of who we are, what we may believe, or what we think we know—1.) WE WILL ALL DIE; 2.) WE WILL ALL BE JUDGED by the Deity for what we have become or by what is available in print and other righteous and spiritual materials. No one is exempted!

The following revelation was taken from the Doctrine and Covenant as revealed to the Prophet Joseph Smith Jr. and Sidney Rigdon on February 16, 1832, which defines the three kingdoms of glory—the lowest, which is the Telestial; the middle, Terrestrial; and the highest, the Celestial into which we will all be relegated except those that are cast out with Satan into outer darkness.

Satan will strive with his billions of followers, both temporal and spiritual, to bring us all down to his level of impending doom in outer darkness. This work defines many of the ways he uses to bring the whole human race down to destruction. His intention never varies and his efforts never cease. Hopefully, this work will help us to not fall into his many traps of deceits and lies.

> (D&C 76:25–35) V 25 And this we saw also, and bear record, that an angel of God who was in authority in the presence of God, who rebelled against the Only Begotten Son whom the Father loved and who was in the bosom of the Father, was thrust down from the presence of God and the Son,
>
> V 26 And was called Perdition, for the heavens wept over him – he was Lucifer a son of the morning!
>
> V 27 And we beheld, and lo, he is fallen! Is fallen even a son of the morning!

> V 28 And while we were yet in the spirit, the Lord commanded us that we should write the vision; for we beheld Satan, that old serpent, even the devil, who rebelled against God and sought to take the kingdom of our God and his Christ
>
> V 29 Wherefore, he maketh **war** with the saints of God, and encompasseth them round about. (Emphasis added)
>
> V 30 And we saw a vision of the sufferings of those with whom he made war and overcame, for thus came the voice of the Lord unto us;
>
> V 31 Thus saith the Lord concerning all those who know my power, and have been made partakers thereof, and suffered themselves through the power of the devil to overcome, and deny the truth and defy my power
>
> V 32 They are they who are the sons of perdition, of whom I say that it had been better for them never to have been born;
>
> V 33 For they are vessels of wrath, doomed to. Suffer the wrath of God, with the devil and his angels in eternity;
>
> V 34 Concerning whom I have said there is no forgiveness in this world nor in the world to come
>
> V 35 Having denied the Holy Spirit after having received it and having denied the Only Begotten Son of the Father, having crucified him unto themselves 'and put him to an open shame.
>
> V 36 These are they who shall go away into the lake of fire and brimstone, with the devil and his angels
>
> V 37 And the only ones on whom he second death shall have any power;

It is imperative that we understand why we are placed here on earth. We must learn to conduct our lives in a manner which will bring us back into the presence of God and his son Jesus Christ. If not, we may belong to Satan.

We cannot hide behind our ignorance when the information for our spiritual growth is available through the scriptures and other good and enlightening books. By ignoring the available information, we cannot expect to receive the same blessings and spiritual advancement as those who embrace and apply the available information. This book was written to aid the readers in their sincere search to increase their spiritual enlightenment. It will also help integrate their lives more harmoniously with others and bring them closer to God.

The true meaning of love and hate is explained in a comprehensive and edifying manner. It leaves no doubt about what is required for our ultimate residence with our Creator.

Satan's true evil purposes and what weapons he uses in his attempts to bring about man's destruction are revealed. God's weapons to combat the terrible influences Satan brings to bear on the human family are also discussed extensively. The meaning of many other unifying traits and characteristics is discussed such as love, charity, humility, and loyalty; also, many of the disunifying traits and characteristics are discussed such as anger, hate, doubt, and greed.

The continual corruption of our spirits by the satanic onslaught of our physical brain also affects our spiritual brain with the production of habits, addictions, phobias, other unwanted characteristics, and attributes and traits which are unacceptable to God and counter to his righteous laws and commandments.

Love is Satan's greatest enemy because it is the glue that holds mankind together. Satan will diminish this love in all of its many forms—it's splendor and beauty—to a thing of naught if we don't or won't magnify and let it grow.

Agency, being next to love in importance, becomes next in line in the necessity of or using it righteously. If we always use it righteously and with force, we won't lose it. We must know that it is being hit with all—of the slings and arrows of that portion of society which has already succumbed to Lucifer's promptings.

In these last days, these two blessings from God, love and agency, will be under attack by the Devil and his billions of spirits and those mortals who follow them in like no other time in the history of this world.

The continual bombardment of our spirits by things that are stimulating, exciting, and seemingly innocuous influences our minds and spirits to develop habits and addictions which are not acceptable to God. Our spirits become inured against that which is good, righteous, and spiritually acceptable; thus, our spirits can become so laden with evils and sin of which we have not repented and will prevent us from entering the Celestial kingdom where God dwells.

Through continual introspection (looking inward) and examining our use of unrighteous traits and characteristics then repenting of them, we will be cleansed and allowed the privilege and the blessings of living with the heavenly Father again.

There is a law irrevocably decreed in heaven before the foundation of the world upon which all blessings are predicated and when any blessing is received of God. It is by obedience to that law upon which it is predicated [D&C 20:30].

Our heavenly Father has prepared the way for us to be taught through the Holy Ghost to be righteous entities unto ourselves, and to act righteously under all circumstances without having to rely on him for every action we encounter all within the bounds of love in traits, characteristics, and attributes. This is the perfection process.

Satan, on the other hand, entices, promises, influences, tempts, and prompts us by using all his wiles to program us to be evil agents unto ourselves and to perpetuate all things evil and destructive—from lies, torture, murder, and massive killings which make humanity miserable like himself. He enjoys making everyone suffer pain and discomfort in every way possible.

Satan begins his plans in our childhood; sometimes, it takes many centuries before his plans are brought to fruition. Promises of power, riches, and enjoyment are supposedly ours if we follow him. When we give him the power, he uses his influences and promptings to those of us who are susceptible to do his evil works of destruction and mayhem on their fellow beings.

God has given us our agency and our spirits to become trainable and accept whichever path we choose—the righteous or the evil one. This life then becomes the school or training ground for our conscious and spirit brains. We are the teachers of our spirits and can teach what the Holy Ghost instructs us to do or what Satan and his minions teach. We, as individuals, cannot blame anyone else for what we have become. Our thoughts or mental actions have selected whichever kingdom we have earned and are assigned at the judgment seat of God. We even earn the possibility of being cast into the outer darkness with Satan.

As long as we are here on earth, this schooling is never over; it is being taught by God or Satan 24/7. All of the information we need to get into any of the kingdoms of God is here on earth, so all we have to do is search for and find it. We should always be aware of what we are teaching our spirits. If we and our spirits become inured to the evils around us and accept them as what we want to become, we will inherit the kingdom we have earned.

Satan is a master salesman, so we should be very careful about what we buy—**happiness or misery**.

We all must go through the fiery furnace of our own afflictions and tribulations. Some will make it through okay, and some won't. Some will not even know they are going or have gone through it. Those who do make it through to the Celestial kingdom will benefit far more than they could ever imagine.

Satan's power lies in convincing those who are susceptible, unwary, unknowledgeable, uninformed, weak; seekers of fun, excitement, power, fame, fortune, and sexual gratification; and the non-religious and ungodly. Habits and addictions are part of his evil attempts to destroy us. In fact, he convinces every accountable person on this planet to do despicable, unacceptable activities that demean and debase us. Some things are very evil and destructive while other acts may be overlooked or appear inconsequential, but they are all designed to attain one or more of his aims. Everything he does that we respond to, in any way, puts us on the road to mental, physical, and spiritual destruction unless we become aware of what he is doing and repent.

Those who recognize what has really occurred and are living righteous lives but have been temporarily deceived will immediately repent. Others who don't recognize that it is Satan's work will inevitably continue to the downward path they have chosen until it is too late.

The key to avoiding his influence is to gain the spiritual knowledge, wisdom, and intelligence required to recognize, through the Holy Ghost, the deceits of Satan, and to stay in a repentant state. The scriptures are the source from which we gain the knowledge we need to make the decisions we need to make, guiding us back to God and Jesus Christ.

CHAPTER ONE

Know Your Enemy

These are two of the many absolutes in this life and beyond regardless of who we are or what we have accepted as truth:

1. **WE WILL ALL DIE;**
2. **WE WILL ALL BE JUDGED; WE MUST ACCOUNT TO OUR CREATOR FOR WHAT WE HAVE BECOME. IT MATTERS NOT WHO WE ARE; ALL THAT REALLY MATTERS IS WHAT WE HAVE OR HAVEN'T DONE OR THOUGHT AND THAT OF WHICH WE HAVE REPENTED. IT DOESN'T MATTER—IF WE BELIEVE IN GOD OR NOT, WE ALL MUST DIE AND HAVE TO FACE AND BE JUDGED BY GOD AND JESUS CHRIST.**

    IT WOULD BE GREAT IF WE ALL BELIEVED AND ACTED ON THIS BELIEF. THIS IS GOD'S WORLD AND IT IS HE TO WHOM WE MUST ALL ANSWER FOR OUR THOUGHTS AND ACTIVITIES.

Life on earth is not about what man can do for man, but what God can and will do for man if we follow and allow him to. Which is better—a man-centered life or a God-centered life? Which has the greater potential for spiritual growth—man to man or man to God and God to man? What part does Satan or Lucifer play in this scenario?

What does God offer to mankind for their obedience? It is eternal life through love and obedience to his laws and commandments and by following the plan of salvation. God also promises eternal happiness in one of his glorious kingdoms if we are worthy. These promises are forever and eternal.

What does Satan offer to man for relenting to his temptations and influences? Yielding to his promises are also forever and eternal. He promises much that he won't or can't deliver you from temporary pleasures, power, riches, adulation, excitement, etc., which result in sin, unhappiness, misery, and destruction. He also offers slavery and subjugation to those who have completely embraced his ways. We will have been completely enticed if we follow his road to excitement, pleasure, fun, and power, etc. We can become leaders of great organizations, rulers of towns, cities, states, countries; attain high positions in governments; or become high-ranking military leaders, rich, famous, or influential. The list of people whom Satan tempts includes every individual who was ever born into this world, including Jesus Christ who never heeded his promptings. Satan's promises always end at death but his influences when acted upon without repentance will last for eternity. The scriptures below encourage us to always stay in a state of repentance. If we don't stay repentant, as indicated below, we may end up suffering with those who rebel against God.

From the Book of Mormon, King Benjamin addresses in Mosiah 2:35–39:

> 35 And also, all that has been spoken by our fathers until now. And behold, also, they spake that, which was commanded them of the Lord; therefore, they are just and true.
>
> 36 And now I say unto you, my brethren, that after ye have known and have been taught all these things, if you should transgress and go contrary to that which has been spoken, that ye do withdraw yourselves from the spirit of the Lord, that it may have no place in you to guide you in wisdom's paths that ye may be blessed, prospered, and preserved—

37 I say unto you, that the man that doeth this, the same cometh out in open rebellion against God; therefore he listeth to obey the evil spirit, and becometh an enemy to all righteousness; therefore, the Lord has no place in him, for he dwelleth not in unholy temples.

38 Therefore if that man repenteth not, and remaineth and dieth an enemy to God, the demands of divine justice do awaken his immortal soul to a lively sense of his own guilt, which doth cause him to shrink from the presence of the Lord, and doth fill his breast with guilt, and pain, and anguish, which flame ascendeth up forever and ever.

39 And now I say unto you, that mercy hath no claim on that man; therefore, his final doom is to endure a never-ending torment.

From this scripture, we see that God has not left us alone to fight the battles with Satan unless we really do completely rebel against him.

God's plan may be more difficult to follow, but the rewards are so much greater that there should never be a question as to which path we should take!

When Lucifer was cast out of heaven with a third of its hosts (God's children), he and his fallen angels became our mortal enemies. He and his minions, then, swore to destroy us mentally, physically, emotionally, and spiritually by using every means at their disposal. It matters not if we are completely spiritual, religious, or if we wholeheartedly embrace all of his wicked ways or even if we worship him as a god—he has still sworn our demise because in the spirit world from which we all came, we would not follow him in his rebellion against God. If we don't rebel in this life and follow God's commandments and laws, we have nothing to worry about, but if we do rebel, we have joined Lucifer's followers. I believe that many times, those who follow Satan don't really know or recognize that the evils we actively pursue come directly or indirectly from Satan and his minions. Satan does not want any recognition for the evils he perpetrates because he wants to remain invisible to us and make it look as if we humans, all by ourselves, plan his atrocities. This makes it much easier for him to create havoc and destruction to our bodies, minds, and spirits.

> (DC 29:36–37) V 36 And it came to pass that Adam, being tempted of the devil—for, behold, the devil was before Adam, for he rebelled against me, saying, Give me thine honor, which is my power; and also a third part of the hosts of heaven turned he away from me because of their agency;
> V 37 **And they were thrust down, and thus came the devil and his angels.**
> (2 Nephi 2:16) The Lord God gave unto man that he should act for himself. Wherefore man could not act for himself save it should be that he was enticed by one or the other;

The Holy Ghost or the satanic forces of evil [my addition]—the conundrum is that scientifically, we cannot prove that Satan exists, let alone prove that he has any influence over us. Our only proof that he or God exists is in the Scriptures and from our modern prophets. The only truth that exists lies in our righteous beliefs and in viewing the grandeur of this world, which God created with its infinite variety of life in the sky above, the ocean depths, and on this earth.

Satan doesn't care how small or how large the indiscretion (sin) or evil which we embrace and act on; he is still behind the perpetration of every evil, either directly or indirectly. These perpetrations may have been of a recent origin or may have been planted in the minds of men hundreds or even thousands of years ago. The evil may be insignificant or enormous, but it is still Satan and his evil spirits or those human followers who have unwittingly or knowingly joined forces with him behind the scenes who is instigating the temptations and the many promises which all result in pain, chaos, violence, torture, mayhem, and death. I estimate that from the number of humans that have ever been on the earth or are now residing here going well over 48 billion, that gives Satan at least 16 billion helpers—a very large number of dedicated evil spirit entities and their living followers to bring about destruction, violence, chaos, and mayhem to the human families.

My nephew Jay Ball concludes that God is not a distant God. He is an immediate and intimate God. We say he knows our thoughts, and that is true enough! That is because he is giving us the ability and the freedom to think. Therefore, he knows how to judge us because everything we have done has used his power. He lends us life and light. We have the freedom to act and choose our *agency*, but *our agency* operates inside a creation powered by and dependent upon God.

For whatever, large or small, evil is taking place in any part of the world and mankind is always the one blamed. Satan, although he is the major perpetrator, seldom if ever gets the credit or responsibility. It is true that those who list to obey Satan are probably punished for what Satan has enticed them to do. This is as it should be because we have used our agency non-righteously. However, no mention is seldom made of the part Lucifer plays in the commission of these heinous crimes and sins. We must accept the fact that we can never punish Satan for what he does; only God can do that, which in my opinion, he won't do until the wheat and the tares have been separated and God's plan for us no longer needs Satan's influence to separate those who follow him from those who follow or who have followed God and his plan of salvation, happiness, and exaltation.

I believe that in our first judgment, when we die, we will be judged by what our previous thoughts and actions have produced—good or evil. These thoughts and actions **determine what we were and are willing to become—Telestial, Terrestrial, or Celestial beings. At the final judgment, Jesus Christ the Supreme Judge will judge everyone that has lived a terrestrial life during the millennium by what we were willing to become—Terrestrial or Celestial beings. Also, being judged are those spirits who have already been judged unworthy to be in the Terrestrial world in which, hopefully, we will soon be living.**

Every thought we have that has produced an evil action is caused by the influence of Satan and his wicked spiritual and physical followers who cannot be punished by those who have become his victims. Every undesirable word, every action that produces any discomfort, or any violence on anyone living—whether it be mild or resulting in physical, mental, or emotional pain, torture, or even death—has been initiated by Satan and his minions or by someone under their control. No one is exempt from these malevolent intrusions.

CHAPTER TWO

The Traits of Evil and Righteousness

Below are listed a few of the many evil, hateful, and fearsome traits, characteristics, and attributes the devil uses to attain his goals of the destruction of our agency, righteousness, and our very lives. Each of these traits can be amplified and magnified by Satan, to the extent that our control may be lost and our actions may result in some terrible or unlawful event which could be disastrous to our freedom and life, and that of others as well.

EVIL TRAITS

ANGER, CARELESSNESS, CHEATING, CONTENTION, CRUELTY, DISHONESTY, DISLOYALTY, DISOBEDIENCE, DESTRUCTION, DOUBT, ENVY, GOSSIP, GREED, GRUDGING, HOSTILITY, HATE, IRREVERENCE, JEALOUSY, LYING, MERCILESSNESS, MALICIOUSNESS, UNREPENTANT, PREJUDICE, PRIDE, RAGE, REVENGE, SHAME, UNCHASTE, UNFORGIVING, NON-PRAYERFUL, UNRIGHTEOUS, UNTEACHABLE, UNTRUSTWORTHY, WEAK, NON-VIRTUOUS, AND MANY MORE.

More traits of evil, hate, and divisiveness are given later in this work.

From a little white lie to the creation of gigantic world wars, Satan is at the helm using the above traits, attributes, characteristics, and many more to guide his henchmen in both physical and spiritual—to create all the havoc, evils, violence, the ravishing of women, torture, etc. His work is not limited to our physical bodies but involves and affects our minds, emotions, and our spirits. His efforts are vast, unforgiving, and unyielding—involving every accountable human born into this world. His efforts have been passed down through the centuries until the present to accomplish his evil designs of our ultimate destruction.

All wars have been well planned by him. The structure of the military forces in every country in the world has been organized by him, from the governments who control the generals to the lowly privates who carry out the killing. Each rank has been designed so as to control those under them and receive orders from those over them. There is no room for disobedience or severe punishment will be meted out, making it mandatory to kill, maim, punish, torture, and create mayhems. The governments under Satan's pressure who control the media create the hatred and the desire through propaganda to kill the enemy. This whole scheme is created by Satan millennia ago with variations in each country involved. This whole system is controlled by force, making it almost impossible not to be obedient to kill and maim. Our agency (the opportunity to choose) is lost. Satan has designed this plan well. Unfortunately, when we're inducted or enlisted in the service of our country, we lose our ability to choose. The responsibility for the killing and mayhem, then, falls on the leaders of the countries who perpetrated the wars. Satan is seldom if ever, blamed or held responsible.

Below are listed a few of the many righteous, loving, and unifying traits, attributes, and characteristics that are, in my opinion, what our Lord and Savior expects us to perfect to the best of our ability in this life. Satan will attempt to diminish or weaken these traits in intensity or to invalidate them entirely if we allow.

LOVE-BASED TRAITS

APPRECIATION, CHARITY, COMMITMENT, COMPASSION, COURAGE, DEDICATION, FAITH, FORGIVENESS, GENTLENESS, GODLINESS, HONESTY, HONOR, HUMILITY, INTEGRITY, JUSTICE, KINDNESS, KNOWLEDGE, LOVE, MEEKNESS, MERCY, MODESTY, MORALITY, OBEDIENCE, REPENTANCE, REVERENCE, RIGHTEOUSNESS, SELF-ESTEEM, SENSITIVITY, SPIRITUALITY, STABILITY, TEMPERANCE, TRUST, TRUTH, AND VIRTUE.

Many more traits of love and unity and those of hate and disunity are itemized later in this composition.

Mankind, as a whole, does not acknowledge that there is a means available to counter the effects of Lucifer's promptings. Seemingly, man will not search the various methods available or what steps can be taken to deter the devil and his angels from their onslaught of mayhem and destruction. Hence, we are doomed to repeat the evils, our misdeeds, and the horrors Lucifer has persuaded us to engage in over and over. Later, there will be a discussion on the many ways and means available to counter Satan's attacks; primarily, I now desire to concentrate on just how Satan is able to accomplish his many atrocities.

CHAPTER THREE

Satan Unveiled

The devil, Satan, or Lucifer (these are the most common of the many names given to the devil) assumes the leadership role of commanding his armies in both physical and spiritual into luring, enticing, deceiving, tempting, and compelling mankind to break and change all of God's laws and commandments. He hopes to destroy us all by isolating us from God's presence, denying God's children the opportunity of repenting and becoming one with God and Jesus Christ in their kingdom.

Satan knows all of God's laws and commandments. He knows our weaknesses—what brings us the most pleasure, fun, excitement, delight, etc. He knows that we are susceptible to the gratification that participating in many evil activities brings us, so he exploits them. Any activity that we humans use to place us ahead of our responsibility to God or at least those that place our desires ahead of God's plans for us should be considered evil or sin. Are we not worshiping our cherished activities and possessions above our desires for living with God? Is this not idol worship?

Looking back on my life, I find that I have been guilty of this very thing. I love to fish, and in my earlier days, I have loved many sports that I placed ahead of my duties and responsibilities to God and my family. I have had to do some repenting!

To name all the methods and ways Satan uses to bring about our downfall, it would take volumes. There are approximately 500 traits, characteristics, attributes, elements, or components of righteousness and love, and about the same amount for unrighteous traits and characteristics of hate, anger, and fear. There are literally hundreds or thousands of situations, events, and circumstances which Satan exploits and uses to make our lives miserable and/or bring us down to ruin and death. Our evil habits and enjoyable activities that we place ahead of our duties to God, family, and humanity are transferred to our spirits. Unless we repent of them, they can eventually become compulsive behavior patterns with which we must live for eternity.

Most of us are blind to the intensity, severity, magnitude, subtlety, and the very depths of Satan's abilities to influence us and accomplish his destructive aims.

It all begins in our minds where most of our thoughts and decisions are being monitored and weighed on very delicate mental, emotional, and spiritual scales. Two forces, God's and Satan's, are mostly present and influence our thoughts, emotions, and actions. Also, each event we experience has the same two forces originally *equal* in intensity and affecting the direction we should take—the righteous or the unrighteous. Our response to whichever influence we choose determines which path we take—good or evil, positive or negative, righteous or unrighteous [there is more to this equation, which will be discussed later].

The direction we take is entirely up to each of us. We cannot say at the judgment seat that Satan's influence was greater than the Holy Ghost's, so we chose this, the wrong path. Satan's influence may have been laced with promises of fun, enjoyment, excitement, power, and wealth which we may choose over the promise of eternal life with the heavenly Father, but the use of our agency makes it our responsibility and no one else's. Our past choices and decision also play a large part in which path we take. If willingly we have taken the wrong path before, it may be easier to take again. We make the choice and must take the responsibility for it, and live with or repent of it. The blame cannot be placed on any other individual or even the devil. We always take the path we desire most because of the lure of the promises involved from both sides—eternal happiness or fun, excitement, and enjoyment for the moment which may entail considerable and painful repentance later on.

Our past choices and decisions may also come from our acceptance of the influence parents, teachers, ecclesiastical leaders, the media, and others have over us. We esteem their knowledge and experience and believe and accept their teachings not realizing that they may have come from the devil many generations before and are now handed down to us in this lifetime. Since we have already chosen the path we're on, the previous decisions we have made make it much easier to take the same path again whether it comes from the Holy Ghost or Satan.

These two influences are always present unless we have completely denied God and his plan of salvation. These influences also affect our thoughts, actions, and emotions, increasing or decreasing their intensity as we allow. If our thoughts list towards evil or any unrighteous activity, extra care should be taken to change before it's too late. If our thoughts lean towards good and righteous activities, we should magnify and expand our efforts to nullify Satan's destructive influences.

We, God's children, should become more and more aware of the powers and the all-out efforts the devil and his followers in both physical and spiritual aspects are resorting to in these last days. Christ will soon be coming again before most of us are ready. *We really need to prepare for the devil's **extended and expanded** efforts to destroy our reliance on God and his plan of salvation and exaltation in these last days.*

The description of the magnitude of satanic evil is beyond any language on earth. There just aren't enough adjectives to do the description with justice. I'll give just one incidence that shows what the devil can tempt us to do.

While serving in the army and I was stationed in Dachau, Germany just after World War II, when the war crimes' trials were proceeding, this horrible incident was presented to the judge and jury where the German medical doctors were doing experiments on how much pain women could endure before death. One terrible incident has bothered me through the years, which occurred when the medical doctors bound the women's legs together who were beginning to deliver a child. There was no relief for them except death, which I'm sure they welcomed whole-heartedly. These women had many electronic devices attached to them which measured pain intensity and seemingly all for the edification of their scientific community.

There were many other atrocities committed by the Germans with which I do not desire to acquaint you. Satan's use of people to torture other people knows no limits. His influence on susceptible and willing people to do his bidding goes beyond my understanding. The atrocities I heard of while serving in Viet Nam were equally horrendous and were also beyond my comprehension. How can Satan influence anyone to do such evils and enjoy the pain, suffering, and devastation he creates?

When one takes into consideration the terrible annihilation of people in many communist countries around the world—20 to 30 million each in China and the Soviet Union—one begins to realize the magnitude of the control Lucifer has over the hearts and minds of the world's populations and its leaders. Because of the evils that existed prior to the flood, every human in the world was destroyed except for eight souls—Noah and his family. When one considers the tremendous organization that must be implemented in creating the terrible satanic influences that perpetrated these mind-boggling evils, it makes one realize that we can't counter them without God's help. He allows these things to happen for reasons we don't always understand.

One of the reasons is to allow Satan to seal for himself those who obey him and rebel against God to their utter destruction [the separation of the wheat and the tares]. God seldom interferes with what man does to a man. I don't pretend to know all of the reasons why God allows or doesn't allow these atrocities to happen. His love, knowledge, intelligence, wisdom, power, glory, and what is needed for our progression toward his kingdom are so far above ours that for us to criticize or question him in any way would be an exercise in futility and could lead to our rebellion against him. No one on this earth has the right to question or criticize any of his actions.

What he does or doesn't do is always for a good reason which we mere mortals must accept or go crazy in trying to understand. One reason mentioned in the scriptures as to why God allows us, mortals, the choice of being sifted (wheat and tares) by multiple experiences is so that we see what path we would eventually choose—the easy one with Satan or the harder one back to God.

All of the destructive abilities of the satanic forces of evil fade in comparison to the awesome and infinitely more powerful forces of God, i.e. his kingdom and his priesthood, which always maintain a balance between these two forces if we allow. Without this balance controlled by God, man would lose his agency—one of the most cherished blessings with which God favors his children here on earth. This balance is absolutely necessary, or we would lose our agency. If the devil's power was greater than God's, we would eternally be controlled by Satan, our agency would be lost, and we would be miserable for eternity. If God's powers were always expressed to a greater extent, we would again lose our agency because we would only have one choice and there would be no way to determine which way our own personas listed. It's our own choices that allow God to determine who should be with him again. It's our decisions that either strengthen or weaken us spiritually. God needs us to be strong so he can trust and depend on us to make the right decisions, which brings more power and glory to his kingdom. This earth-life is the training ground to determine the eternal road we will travel—up or down.

CHAPTER FOUR

Satan's Enemy

The big question that really needs to be answered is—are we enemies to Satan or are we so caught up in his world of enticements and promises that we can't be bothered? Are we just too busy to understand the gravity of our decisions? Maybe we have already joined his forces!

We all should be Satan's enemies since he is continually striving to destroy each one of us and make us miserable like he is. **We really need to acknowledge that he is at war with us.** If we are to survive and attain the highest degree of glory in God's kingdom, we must declare and wage a winning war against Lucifer and his legions here on earth with guidance from God, our Lord Jesus Christ, and the Holy Ghost.

We are definitely not alone in this war against Satan because we can always rely on the powers of God and his army of helpers. The battles with Satan will be much easier if we have been obedient to God's laws and commandments, and more difficult if we fall toward Lucifer's temptations. Our selection determines which side we choose, God's or Satan's. The tools we alone choose to study or not and the instructions we receive will help put us on the right or wrong path. We will not be judged by what everyone else has thought or done that has influenced our decisions—only on what we have accepted from them and what we read and study. When we make our decisions based on the input we receive without verifying their authenticity, we are definitely held responsible. Should this not put a great amount of influence on what we read, hear, and accept on our selection of the material we choose as truth?

Shouldn't we study our enemy more closely and recognize how he uses people from all walks of life regardless of race color, intelligence, or any biases, or for any other reason, to do his bidding? Shouldn't we as nations, states, counties, cities, towns, organizations, and families learn to identify each of his deceits, his lies, how he controls our emotions, and exactly how he plans our destruction? We must understand that it is he who creates in our hearts and minds all of the commotions, contentions, atrocities, wars, mayhems, strife, bigotries, prejudices, hatred, greed, anger, and all the other destructive traits and characteristics, **and intensifies them.** If he succeeds, he will make us slaves to do his bidding and accomplish his evil designs. He can also control and change our emotions by diminishing our righteous traits and magnifying those that are unrighteous to support his objectives.

We should never become passive or complacent and recognize instead the power we allow Satan to have over us. He is using his powers every second of every day to gradually bring us directly and indirectly under his control *if we permit.* To minimize his efforts, we need to develop righteous plans of action based on our knowledge of the scriptures and the revealed word of our modern prophets. God's eternal plan of salvation should be one of our major goals. God does not intend that we fight this war alone. In humility, we need to rely on his help through prayer, and by his priesthood, to identify each of Satan's efforts so we can choose the righteous path and ultimately win our independence from him.

The only real entity between us and the kingdom of God is Lucifer and his minions who never sleep nor take a break or vacation. He is absolutely relentless and is dedicated to our demise, never giving up. When we completely realize this, we can and should always rely on our Savior to understand and to depend entirely on his great power to assist us in overcoming all of Satan's temptations, his plans for us, his promptings, and influences.

God will never interfere with our agencies (our right to choose). He will and has given us the tools necessary to **detect and discern** all of Lucifer's ploys and deceptions, so shouldn't we, then, learn to listen to and heed God's promptings and influences to counter Satan's objectives? Our big problem is that we can't seem to recognize each and every subterfuge, duplicity, and scam Satan uses to mislead, manipulate, and trick us into doing his bidding. Again, he is relentless and never sleeps or takes a vacation—*pure and simple—but he and his hoards are completely and totally evil, determined, and dedicated to make us evil and achieve our downfall.*

Just how does Satan succeed in bringing his devastations and disasters on us?

I don't like to use the term telepathy, so I'll use mind-to-mind communication. We all have a body in which dwells an eternal spirit. Satan and his hoards are all spirits, so there is communication between them and our spirits. The Holy Ghost is also a spirit as are the billions of righteous spirits who also connect with us in a spirit-to-spirit communication. Our minds, spirits, and our emotions are Satan's targets and are what we use to control our actions. Choosing between righteous and unrighteous actions is our major problem. The Holy Ghost and Satan or one of his aides help us make up our minds to use or not to use the mental images they both create. Do we lean toward the satanic forces which entice us with promises of excitement, fun, power, and enjoyment or the righteous powers of God who promises us eternal life and happiness with him in his kingdom? **The choice is always ours!**

Lucifer cannot be in more than one place at a time, so he uses his billions of willing spiritual helpers and those living helpers to bring us down to his level. I believe that he assigns at least one of his evil helpers to each member of the human race, especially to church members so that the temple can recommend holders to carry out his plan of torture, destruction, mayhem, and wickedness. The communication system he uses is a mind-to-mind activity which is very similar to our radio waves. I believe that his organization is extremely complex, efficient, and thoroughly capable of carrying out his orders and objectives—the torture and utter destruction of humankind.

Fortunately, God has an even greater organization—his priesthood here on earth and in heaven—all righteous members of the human race and in the spirit world with which we are all involved. God's infinite power, if we let it, counters the devil's power. Every human being on earth is involved in one way or the other with God's organization. The Holy Ghost and God's angels are the generals in the spirit world and our prophets here on earth are our generals subject to orders from our Master, Jesus Christ. The church, priesthood leaders, and the rest of the church membership and all righteous humans make up the army here on earth to fight the battles with the devil and his minions. In the spirit world, those who are worthy and trained are assigned to us as ***our own personal guardian angels*** to protect us in all ways if we allow—physically, mentally, emotionally, and spiritually. They also make a record of all of our thoughts and actions, good and bad. I believe that these assignments are made according to our needs and worthiness. After baptism, we have the gift of the Holy Ghost conferred on us by the priesthood which provides us with the constant companionship of our own personal ***guardian angel*** who tries to keep us from sinning and being in trouble [my opinions in bold and italics].

CHAPTER FIVE

The Scale and Extent of Satan's Forces

To understand the magnitude of Satan's efforts, we should examine the great evils that have befallen mankind through the ages by looking at both the great and small evils that exist in our world today. Who perpetrated the evils that led to the necessity of the flood in Noah's time? Look at Sodom and Gomorrah and at the mass destruction of the Jews by Hitler. Evaluate the terrible destruction of human life when communism came into being in all of the communist nations. Take a good look at the terrorist countries in the world today. Do we enjoy these great evils? Who planned them? What can we do about those which are occurring in the world today? Why are we so vulnerable and gullible to Satan's promptings? It is not because we love misery, but maybe we have not yet learned how to respond correctly to Satan's promptings and influences or that we don't recognize the difference between good and evil! Perhaps, we have not seriously considered the teachings of our Savior. Maybe, we haven't learned how to recognize good thoughts from evil thoughts or that we don't realize that we will be judged by our thoughts as well as our actions and what we have become. Maybe we haven't bothered to learn each of the devil's method of attack—how he operates. Often, we don't even know our own areas of vulnerability. Many of us won't acknowledge that we respond to the devil to any significant degree, especially those of us who are under his control or we may not even believe that we are at war with him. Is it too painful for us to admit that we are often fighting on his side when we sin? To do so may be too much for us to accept, so we just ignore and try to justify our actions by lame and invalid excuses. So, we become his puppets, his dupes, or his soldiers doing his bidding all because we just can't be bothered to take the steps that God has outlined in the scriptures to protect us from the powers of evil. Perhaps, we have not yet learned to hear and heed the whisperings of the Holy Spirit and take the righteous course of action.

We react when Satan influences someone to emotionally, mentally, or physically harm us. We often allow Satan to magnify our emotions out of proportion and out of control. He prompts us to give in to greed, anger, rage, hatred, lust, loud and lewd language, etc. He increases the magnitude of other destructive traits, even our selfish desires. Often, we allow him the power that entices us to ignore and cast aside the teachings of our parents, our churches' leaders, and our society for the pleasures, excitement, power, and the wealth of the world. Many of us become fun seekers, gamers, gratification-minded procrastinators, or lustful sex seekers. Many of us are passive to the evils that surround us in the world. Our satanically induced complacency is necessary so we won't have to acquire the courage to take the necessary steps to change our path toward spirituality and harmony. Why do we heed Satan so often and so easily? Is it because he makes it acceptable, attractive, and enjoyable? This enjoyment is only a facade that hides the misery of disobedience.

Looking back on the major wars of my lifetime, I'm 92-plus years old, and I am amazed at the gullibility of the general public of all nations. We all stand ready and willing to believe anything and everything the media and our governments feed us. The lies, deceits, and propaganda we so readily accept and react to cannot come from God.

The media makes it so easy and acceptable to kill and torture other human beings all for the power and greed of those behind the scenes who completely embrace evil. This is Satan's work to use people as weapons and tools to destroy each other. Why do we consistently let the media and our governments do this to us? Will we never learn?

History has given us this lesson for thousands of years and we still haven't learned. War was never created to protect us from another nation although at times, we must. War was created by the greedy to get gain and power over others. Those who use war to get money and power to satisfy their greedy natures realize that we must protect ourselves from others and so they exploit this knowledge for their own evil purposes. We, as citizens of all nations, become victims and dupes in these great perpetrations of evil. We are pawns and so we reap the diseases, pains, death, and destruction that should by lot fall on those powers behind the scenes of the governments which are responsible for the wars and bloodsheds because of satanic manipulations. In essence, though, it is Satan who magnifies the greed and selfishness in those who use us. These powers behind the governments do not realize that they are losing far more than we who are their puppets.

Looking back on my 24-plus years in the army, I now realize that each grade advancement was a necessary promotion to keep me in the service and further the aims of the greedy so they can get richer and have more power. This realization is something I must repent of and live with for what few years I have left on this earth. I now know that this charade is a ploy of Satan to keep people in the service to further his aims of mayhem, torture, and destruction. The complexity of the armies of the world was created by Lucifer and his hoards.

Each of us, personally, is responsible for his own salvation, spiritual growth, and progress here on earth, and when we choose to respond to the promptings and influences of Satan, to any extent, we are lost except for the blessing of repentance. The rewards for the greedy and their great evils bring them nothing but temporary wealth and power while they are here on earth. At death, these perks are lost to them, along with the opportunity to reside with God throughout the eternities. The reward for being totally evil is eternal misery with no hope. Is eternal punishment worth the power and wealth gained in this short lifetime? I think not. **Of course, there** *is always repentance to begin the long, hard path back to God. The excuse of not being aware that God exists or of the eternal consequences of sinning does not hold water because God's word has been present on earth since Adam and Eve and the ability to search for the truth existed.*

CHAPTER SIX

The Conflict Goes On

All great military leaders agree on one thing—before they can win a war against their enemies, they first must get to know them. They study their strategies, learn their weaknesses, their strengths, when, where, and how to find them, and what weapons and devices are most effective against them.

We really need to realize that Satan and his billions of evil spirits are our only true enemies so we need to direct our energies and strategies accordingly. Our generals then learn how many troops the enemy has, where they are located, and what strengths they have. In short, they learn everything about the enemy that is available. The same things should be done as we fight against the evil forces, which will destroy us if we don't take the steps to know our enemies as they know us.

Our energies should be channeled into increasing our love for God and for our fellowmen regardless of who they are. *Love and all of its traits, attributes, and characteristics are among the greatest weapons God has given us to fight against Satan. Love is God's ultimate law and weapon; those who cherish and use it righteously create little islands of peace, strength, tranquility, and power in the world. It helps to allay the evils and unrighteousness surrounding us.*

Satan's attempt to destroy us never ceases. Our efforts to prevent his destruction also should never cease. We ought to be on guard against his onslaught in every wakeful moment. When hurts and fits of anger swell within us, we should realize from whence they come. Until we do, we will vent our frustrations and anger on those we love. At that moment, we are acting as the devil's henchmen. It is easy to respond to anger with anger or to hatred with hatred. When God commanded us to love our enemies, I believe he was telling us to respond to these evil situations with love and kindness, not retaliation. "Vengeance is mine, I will repay, saith the Lord," in Romans 12:19.

Whose side are we on when we respond to anger with anger or hatred with hatred, etc.? Certainly, not God's! Only he can punish the devil, not us. God's eternal punishment will not occur until after the millennium when the devil is chained and cast into outer darkness with his spiritual and resurrected followers. Since Lucifer is aware of God's ultimate plans for his fate, he uses his free reign to do anything he wishes to the inhabitants of this world. Our only hope is to rely completely on the Deity for strength, faith, love, hope, charity, courage, knowledge, wisdom, and intelligence to cope with the evils of Satan and his followers in his last days on earth until the millennium is over. He will then be released to tempt those who were born during the millennium and test their thoughts and actions; what they have become physically, mentally, and spiritually; and whom they list to follow, God or Satan.

When the thousand years are ended, Satan shall be loosed, men again shall begin to deny their God, and rebellion shall well up in the hearts of many. For a little season, the devil will be free to gather together his armies, even the hosts of hell, and then the final battle will be fought in which Satan (who is perdition) with all his sons shall be cast out forever. (D. & C. 29:22-29, 43:31; 88:119–115; Rev. 20:7-10; 2 Ne. 9:16) Then will come the end of the earth as it is now constituted for it will attain its final destiny as a celestial sphere and the meek shall inherit it forever. (D. & C. 88:16-20)

It is interesting to note the progression of disagreement under the influence of Satan is thus—a disagreement between people created by Satan will be inflated into anger, then into rage, on into hatred, and may then generate an evil, destructive action. This same scenario is repeated with many other evil traits.

Many of us believe that Satan only prompts us to sin, but we must also realize that he magnifies our destructive emotions such as lust, greed, envy, anger, and all other unrighteous traits and characteristics. He also diminishes and retards our righteous traits and characteristics. He is relentless in this pursuit. When we get miffed at someone, if we let him, he will magnify it into hatred which may lead to our doom if we don't stop him. He will also expand his efforts to dampen and diminish the love, compassion, humility, and all other righteous traits, so they will have less of an effect on their recipients. Don't ever be fooled into believing that Satan has little power over us. Only he and the henchmen he has recruited from the human family will have us believe this. His power over us diminishes as we become more and more righteous and recognize that it is we who allow his power to affect us.

I wish to inject a scripture here from Prophet Joseph Smith's translation of Matthew 1:38–46:

> V 38 Now learn a parable of the fig-tree. When its branches are yet tender, and it begins to put forth leaves, you know that summer is at hand;
>
> V 39 So likewise, mine elect, when they shall see all these things, they shall know that he is near, even at the doors;
>
> V 40 But at that day, and hour, no one knoweth; no, not the angels of God in heaven, but my Father only,
>
> V 41 *But as it was in the days of Noah, so it shall be also at the coming of the Son of Man;*
>
> V 42 *For it shall be with them, as it was in the days, which were before the flood; for until the day that Noah entered into the ark they were eating and drinking, marrying and giving in marriage;*
>
> V 43 *And knew not until the flood came, and took them all away; so shall also the coming of the Son of Man be.*

> V 44 *Then shall be fulfilled that which is written, that in the last days, two shall be in the field, the one shall be taken and the other left;*
> V 45 *Two shall be grinding at the mill, the one shall be taken, and the other left;*
> V 46 *And what I say unto one, I say to all men; watch, therefore, for you know not at what hour your Lord doth come.* (**Emphasis added**)

These scriptures should let us know that there is hope for all of God's children through repentance and sustained endurance to the end. Satan can be beaten only if we follow God's commandments and laws, especially the commandment "love the Lord thy God and love thy neighbor".

To give a brief discussion of just one event that helps us understand the power Satan wields in his intention to destroy an individual—the Prophet Joseph Smith had seen a vision of God the Father and his Son Jesus Christ and after the news got around, the persecution began.

> (The Pearl of Great Price—Joseph Smith History verse 61)
> The excitement, however, still continued, and rumor with her thousand tongues was all the time employed in circulating falsehoods about my father's family, and about myself. If I were to relate a thousandth part of them, it would fill up volumes. The persecution, however, became so intolerable that I was under the necessity of leaving Manchester, and going with my wife to Susquehanna County, in the State of Pennsylvania. While preparing to start—being very poor, and the persecution so heavy upon us that there was no probability that we would ever be otherwise—in the midst of our afflictions, we found a friend in a gentleman by the name of Martin Harris, who came to us and gave me fifty dollars to assist us on our journey [Mr. Harris was a resident of Palmyra Township, Wayne County, in the State of New York, and a farmer of respectability].

This persecution continued until the Prophet Joseph was finally martyred in the Carthage jail in Illinois. One would think that all of the spiritual leaders in the area would be glad that he had seen a vision and get behind Joseph Smith and help him along the way, but these leaders were the first ones to persecute the future prophet. *It is interesting that religious leaders would give in to Satan's promptings so readily, but they did so and still do in many places.* Satan is alive and well equipped to carry on his evil designs of our destruction, especially in these days just before Christ's second coming.

Against Satan and his minions, our battle never ends, but there are some things we can do to help win this war.

When we win a battle against anger, prejudice, and other destructive traits, Satan would have us believe that we have won the war. He will then lull us into a false sense of security by easing up on those areas, then quietly go to another weakness we have left unguarded. If we allow it, he will slowly drag us down to destruction. He is so efficient that many times, we won't even realize we are being attacked until it is too late. Repentance is our only hope when we realize we have relented to Satan's persuasions.

Satan's greatest tools and weapons are his organization, patience, and persistence. He will never give up regardless of who we are. His efforts start even before we reach the age of accountability and do not cease until we die. He works on our parents, our friends, teachers, our peers, and everyone with whom we come in contact, even our enemies, to bombard us with his unholy influences. Subtly, he tries to make acceptable every vice and destructive trait known to man. Absolutely nothing is sacred to him. **He is at war with us, and anything and everything goes.** So, what can we do to counter this everlasting evil onslaught?

We certainly cannot do it alone! We must rely on the only source available—God's plan of salvation, the gospel of Jesus Christ.

We can't kill Satan or injure him in any. He isn't affected by anything the human race can do to him, so our only hope is the intervention of God, Jesus Christ, and the Holy Ghost through earnest prayer and supplication, living the gospel, and being honest and obedient at all times and in all places to God's laws and commandments.

The magnitude of the law of love cannot be overplayed nor should it be underplayed. Its basic premise is that we are never enemies of each other regardless of the situation that presents itself. I know this is hard to accept when our lives or our loved one's lives are being threatened by someone, but we must look past the threat and realize that it is Satan behind the scene that has created the situation. "Vengeance is mine; I will repay," saith the Lord in Romans 12:19.

To so-purify ourselves that we react only with love, and compassion to any situation that comes into our lives is the ultimate aim of those who would be perfect. Relying on the Holy Spirit and having faith in the Deity can see us through any event or experience that may arise in this life. Protecting our family, friends, and those we love may entail some violence to those who will not heed our entreaties, but we need to make sure we are doing what we have to do with God's help and approval as it is very important to our status with him.

The tendency to fight fire with fire is one of our big problems. As mentioned above, **we tend to fight anger with anger, prejudice with prejudice, or hatred with hatred, etc.** An eye for an eye went out with Christ's teachings. How much better and less traumatic it is to fight anger with love, hatred with love, or prejudice with love, etc. God has never told us it would be easy to follow his path; only that it is necessary if we desire to gain residence with him in his kingdom. It is important to remember that the only thing standing between our love and friendship for one another is the enmity placed there by Satan. He gives us millions of excuses to not love one another—just excuses, not reasons. Most of the time, there are no valid reasons for not loving others but thousands of good reasons **to love one another**. We are all brothers and sisters because God is our spiritual Father.

If we, as the human race, could only recognize that Satan and his evil hoards are responsible for most of the pain and suffering in the world and use the weapons God has given us to conquer the evil one, we could almost completely eliminate the misery in the world.

Satan is fully armed and committed to our destruction—physically, mentally, emotionally, and spiritually. He will spare no effort and will use any tool or weapon in his arsenal, including many of us, when we permit, to bring about our physical, mental, emotional, and spiritual demise. His helpers are the third of the hosts of heaven—the fallen angels and those of us who follow him—and are equally dedicated to our destruction. If he has his way, not one of us will be spared. His greatest targets are our agency, all righteous characteristics, traits, attributes, talents, and the magnification of those unrighteous traits and attributes that destroy us to diminish and retard our righteous traits, attributes, and characteristics. We should never let our guards down and allow him the pleasure of our destruction.

If we believe that Satan's forces are in chaos, we should look at the tremendous organization he has which inflicts the pain and suffering that exists or has ever existed in every person in every country in the world since before Adam and Eve. The organization Christ has is not to be discounted which offsets and counters Lucifer's organization if only we let him. One big problem in this world is that, in general, we appear to listen to Satan more than we do to Christ. Remember the flood where the world listened to Satan more than to God's prophets.

Many people use the excuse that "the devil made me do it". The devil doesn't make us do anything; he just entices us to do his bidding by his minions of evil spirits and those of other mortals who have fallen under his spell. We just haven't used our agencies righteously. This agency is a sacred gift from God given to every living human who has ever lived on earth. It is our responsibility to use it righteously; not Satan's evil way.

Two of the many absolutes in this world which are possibly the most important of all absolutes are death and God's judgment of us. It matters not what we believe; these two events will happen. That being the case, we should follow his laws and commandments, and not Satan's promptings.

It is my belief that Satan creates many of our limitations and God helps us remove them.

We are born with some limitations. God helps us to remove them when he knows that he can trust us to use their available powers righteously, productively, and when we have learned the laws involved.

CHAPTER SEVEN

The Battle Continues

Another of Satan's major goals is to destroy our physical bodies. He does this in many ways such as influencing those in our food industry to put additives, dyes, flavor enhancers, destructive chemicals, etc., into our foods, as well as by putting additives like plenty of chlorine and fluorine into our water supplies. Genetically Modified Organisms (GMO's) are used to alter God's natural food supplies which ultimately leads to many of our current ailments. The devil encourages us not to study nutrition. He does not want us to know which foods keep us healthy. He wants us to put our faith in the arm of man about everything including nutrition and religion. After all, businessmen are not interested in attaining wealth; they are just interested in our health, right? How can we expect to remain healthy if we do not study the laws of nutrition and health?

Our educational system should be empowered to teach good nutrition, but Satan will do his utmost to prevent this and influence our academia to teach their students how to alter our food supply for his goal of our misery and destruction. Relying on man and not God for our health would be good if a man was always righteous in his desires to keep us healthy, happy, and wise, but there are those who love money more than our good health by Satan's influences. Relying on man instead of God for good health shows where our faith lies.

For the obedience of every law, there is a blessing! Obedience to the laws of health can prevent many of the functional illnesses in the world today. Information is available to prevent most of our illnesses; we just need to search for it and act on the healthful material we find. It is not hard to be misled by some of the books available on the market and by the very doctors that are supposed to help us be healthy. However, we have the Lord on our side to help us if we will only listen to him.

We also have the Word of Wisdom which he gave to man to keep us healthy. If we study and follow it closely, it will not only help us remain healthy but will help us overcome many of the diseases we have accumulated by disobedience to the laws of health. If we really want to see Satan at work, just look at the world's health field, drugs, alcohol, tobacco, and all other addictions. We not only allow Satan to do it to us but in many cases, we even encourage him to.

God's gift of faith can also be used against Satan. To receive this gift, we must be worthy and in a spiritual state in which we know that God can trust us to use it wisely, righteously, productively, and to help ourselves and others.

The big question is—have I conducted my life in a manner in which God can trust me to use it wisely, productively, and righteously?

When we put our faith in medications, in the AMA, or other leaders of our health organizations in preference to using the great natural healing powers of God, we show where our faith lies.

One comment on the Word of Wisdom—I believe it was given to man as a base from which to begin our search for health and well-being, not as the ultimate word on the subject. There have been so many drugs, remedies, concoctions, and additives that we take into our bodies that it would be impossible to name them all. God wants us to use our knowledge, wisdom, and intelligence to learn all we can about the prescribed drugs, foods, herbs, vitamins, and supplements that we so readily take into our bodies. We must, with wisdom and intelligence, control our own health and well-being, but we should also rely on God to help us do so. *When we put our faith in medications and other healing agents of man in preference to using the great healing powers of God through his priesthood and faith, we definitely need to look where our faith lies.*

God has never left us to fight this war alone. The scriptures show us what weapons are effective in defeating Satan. They were ordained for our use. Man has no weapons other than those God has given him. Let us allow God to be our general in this terrible war Satan is waging against us. We can curb his effectiveness and win in no other way—our salvation and exaltation depends on it.

It is my opinion that Satan would have us believe that if we obey his promptings, we will have more power over people, be happier, and have more joy, fun, and pleasure that we can get by retaliation. He would have us believe that hurting or torturing someone will give us power over them and that doing so will bring us much pleasure. He will try to convince us that increasing an argument to anger, then to rage and hate, will give us power over someone or will make it acceptable bringing harm or even death to the person, thinking that it will justify and assuage our hatred and anger. This same scenario plays out well for Satan's use of many evil traits, characteristics, and attributes.

I don't believe Satan can directly take our lives. However, indirectly, he can certainly shorten it by influencing us to pollute our minds and bodies with pornography, drugs, alcohol, tobacco, overeating, etc. He can also influence us to commit murder and mayhem by causing us to lose control of our tempers—by allowing anger, greed, hate, and other unrighteous traits to control our lives. I believe Satan uses anger and hate more often than any of the other traits to accomplish his evils. A little disagreement breeds anger, which leads to rage and hate, which then can control us to do Satan's bidding. It is easier to pit one faction of humanity against another using anger, hate, bias, and prejudice as the means to instigate these great evils. He pits neighbor against neighbor because of their differences in religion, race, education, countries, states, communities, etc. Hate and bias can pit family against family, even one family member against another member. This hatred is often carried on for generations, bringing suffering and even death to the participants. The devil loves to continue these feuds or differences by inflating the hatred and bias in a way beyond what is normal.

Whether we admit it or not, this war *between good and evil has been going on for thousands of years.* Choosing which side we will fight on is not just a one-time choice. It is a choice we must remake every second of every minute of every day. It is a choice we make for the continuation of every thought that comes into our minds. If the thought is counter-productive to our spiritual growth and we continue to pursue it, we have chosen which side of the war on which we are fighting for in that specific period of time. The more often we choose the wrong thoughts to pursue, the easier it becomes to relent the next time; eventually becoming an addiction. Slowly, we are drawn into a web of sin to which we soon become slaves. We become Satan's soldiers to be used at his discretion, not ours. Satan's aim is to pit mankind against mankind. His spiritual army cannot be killed as can our army. His defeat can only come by diminishing his power by our love, faith, righteousness, and by consistently turning to God in prayer and supplication for his sustaining strength until the devil's power over us no longer exists. Our solution is to rely only on God for the courage and strength to take the steps of repentance.

It is my opinion that most of us are not attentive enough to not allow Satan's influence on us to do his bidding. We're not as vigilant or aware enough of what Satan is trying to do to us because he wants us to believe that he isn't responsible for what we do. We should always be alert to his intrusions. Recognizing and giving in to Satan's promptings instead of God's will certainly be our downfall unless we repent.

We are at war—a war that most of us won't admit to or recognize. It is a one-sided war because, as a whole, we don't take the time or make the effort to understand what this life is all about. Many of us don't want to hear about it; we don't have the time to be bothered. Even as members of God's true church, we are not as knowledgeable as we should be about this war in which we're engaged. Many of us won't develop the weapons we need to fight a winning battle. We don't even bother to find out which weapons are available or effective to nullify Satan's onslaught. Many of us get so caught up in our own little worlds of fun, games, sports, excitement, and gratifications that we refuse to see what's going on.

Lucifer, son of the morning, the fallen angel, the ruler of the kingdom of Hades, has taken the time to know our **weaknesses** and create new ones. He and his minions have learned how to fight the battles against each of us. Are we, then, to let him win the fight without generating the greatest opposition of which we are capable? Will he let us alone if we don't fight back? Not on our eternal lives, he won't! He is dead serious about what he is doing to us. Let us be just as serious and carry the fight to his side for a change.

The book of Alma from the Book of Mormon, chapter 5 verses 19–27 says:

> V 19 I say unto you, can you look up to God at that day with a pure heart and clean hands? I say unto you, can you look up, having the image of God engraven upon your countenances?
>
> V 20 I say unto you, can ye think of being saved when you have yielded yourselves to become subjects of the devil?
>
> V 21 I say unto you, ye will know at that day that ye cannot be saved; for there can no man be saved except his garments are washed white; yea, his garments must be purified until they are cleansed from all stain, through the blood of him of whom it has been spoken by our fathers, who should come to redeem his people from their sins.
>
> V 22 And now I ask of you, my brethren, how will any of you feel, if ye shall stand before the bar of God, having your garments stained with blood and all manner of filthiness? Behold, what will these things testify against you?
>
> V 23 Behold will they not testify that ye are murderers, yea, and also that ye are guilty of all manner of wickedness?
>
> V 24 Behold my brethren do ye suppose that such an one can have a place to sit down in the kingdom of God, with Abraham, with Isaac, and with Jacob, and also all the holy prophets, whose garments are cleansed and are spotless, pure and white?

> V 25 I say unto you, Nay; except ye make our Creator a liar from the beginning, or suppose that he is a liar from the beginning, ye cannot suppose that such can have place in the kingdom of heaven; but they shall be cast out for they are the children of the kingdom of the devil.
>
> V 26 And now behold, I say unto you, my brethren, if ye have experienced a change of heart, and if ye have felt to sing the song of redeeming love, I would ask, can ye feel so now?
>
> V 27 Have. ye walked, keeping yourselves blameless before God? Could ye say, if ye were called to die at this time, within yourselves, that ye have been sufficiently humble? That your garments have been cleansed and made white through the blood of Christ, who will come to redeem his people from their sins?

Satan will go to another ruse when we resist any of his temptations or do a charitable deed for someone. Every time we accomplish or reach a productive goal, visualize his discomfort and the joy of our heavenly Father. Each righteous act will help to reinforce our commitment and dedication to our war against the evil one. Being of service and helping one another would be very advantageous to us in helping combat the satanic forces around us.

It is not enough to just skim the methods, tools, and weapons Satan uses against us, so **we must study with all our hearts and meditate on these things.** Each of us individually and all of us collectively are involved in this war. None of us are excluded, and although many of us have already joined forces with him, it is never too late to repent and switch to the side of those who will ultimately win if we then, endure to the end. If we die without repentance, we may be lost.

Influencing us through anger, greed, hate, and other evil traits to emotionally traumatize others and debase them and then convince people that there is no harm in so doing, is a tactic Satan frequently uses. He then creates within us a sadistic pleasure in perpetrating these evil actions.

This war is real and deadly. Just because we hear no bombs exploding or shots being fired does not mean it should be taken lightly, or we will lose. There have been far too many casualties so far; let us not be next.

Our *generals* in this war are our church leaders, our current prophet, his councilors, the Quorum of the Twelve Apostles, and all the other church's general authorities and leaders including those in our Stakes, Wards, and Branches. *Let us follow these leaders who have been called by God to help us defeat the devil! Of course, ultimately, through the priesthood, their orders come from God and Christ, which are then passed on to his prophets and to all of our Priesthood leaders in the various auxiliaries by the Holy Ghost. If the Christian world would only come together as a force dedicated toward teaching the essentials in fighting Satan and his minions, we could be a righteous force Jesus Christ would be proud of.*

CHAPTER EIGHT

God's Expectations For Us

Sometimes, God allows us to err then shows us the error of our ways so he can more effectively strengthen us and put us on the path back to him and help us to choose the right path the next time and also to repent. God knows that by overcoming our trials and tribulations, we gain spiritual strength. The more often we choose the right path (without Father enabling us), the closer we come to the perfection commanded of us in Matthew 5:48, "Be ye therefore perfect, even as your Father, which is in heaven is perfect."

God has said we should be about doing good without his having to command us in all things. The more righteous we become without the Lord having to command us, the more we become perfected. When we no longer need to be commanded to be righteous because we are already as perfect as Father, we are ready to inherit his kingdom, be one with him, and be like him in every aspect of his glory; then, we will be with him for eternity. However, this does not mean that we don't need his guidance or that we need not pray or study the scriptures—only that we should do these things out of love and charity not because we have to be commanded to [this is my opinion].

We will no longer have to be taught in things pertaining to righteousness because we will have passed the final tests to be with God.

As we progress towards perfection, we will no longer heed Satan with the help and power of God. When that time arrives, we will have finally overcome, conquered, and risen above all adversities and maladies; conquered our evil traits, attributes, and characteristics; and have accepted and magnified our love-based traits, characteristics, and attributes. Only then can we be perfected, have all knowledge, wisdom, intelligence, power, glory, and faith, have the right to a celestial body, and live with God throughout all eternity.

This does not mean that we haven't needed or required Father's help along the way—only that we have needed it less and less as we have traveled the bumpy road to perfection. We, then, will be given all that God has and will be as glorious as Father. We will completely be in harmony with him and will respond to all of his desires. We will finally be one with him and with his son Jesus Christ.

This earth life is not about what man wants from man or what man can do for man, but what God wants and can do for a man. If a man obeys man, he has no hope; Satan plans it that way. If a man follows God's plan for man, his hope is sure, and we can live with him forever.

CHAPTER NINE

The Powers and Influences of Satan

Satan has great power and control over all sports, music, gaming, sex, the newspaper media, television, the movie industry, agriculture, GMO's, and anything to take our minds off our path to righteousness and perfection. In fact, every aspect of our lives including our work environments, our medical industry, food industry, etc., are all his targets. There is no place on earth that is safe from the satanic influences of every type of evil, except for our Holy Temples. If the world population spent only a fraction of its time on righteous endeavors instead of frivolous or evil activities, we would all be better prepared to meet our Savior when he comes to cleanse the world. This doesn't mean we should give up the things we enjoy—only that we be moderate and not place those enjoyments in preference to God's plans for us. If we play golf, go fishing, hunting, etc., instead of attending our church meetings and other assigned responsibilities, we are relenting to Satan's temptations above our church duties. Striving for excellence in sports or any other activities is part of growing spiritually if we are attempting to draw closer to God in so doing, but when we do these things for our own personal gratification and excluding God from the equation, they may bring troubles we may not need.

Satan's forces influence us to invent ways and means to take our minds off God's plans for us.

(II Corinthians 11:11–15)
V 11 Wherefore? Because I love thee not? God knoweth.
V 12 But what I do, that I will do, that I may cut off occasion from them which desire occasion; that wherein they glory, they may be found even as we.
V 13 For such are false apostles, deceitful workers, transforming themselves into the apostles of Christ.
V 14 ***And no marvel; for Satan himself is transformed into an angel of light;***
V 15 ***Therefore it is no great thing if his ministers also be transformed as the ministers of righteousness; whose end shall be according to their works.*** (**Emphasis added**)

This shows that the power of Satan is beyond what most of us can comprehend. If Satan and his minions can transform themselves into angels of light, then we must rely on the Holy Ghost to reveal Satan and his minions for what they truly are—absolute evil. Perhaps, he can also transform himself into a false human form, so who, then, can deceive us even more? We must always be on guard against these intrusive evils, which may lead us down to destruction.

It stands to reason that if God's kingdom has the ultimate righteous power in the universe, then Satan's power in his kingdom is the greatest unrighteous evil power on earth. Since God's power is much greater than Satan's, his power is the ruling power in the universe. If this were not so, all humanity would be consigned to the devil's kingdom where no progress would ever be forthcoming. Then why do so many of us choose Satan's way over God's way?

We are all aware that Satan uses his dupes to bring pain, suffering, and misery into the world. We are reluctant to admit that he often uses us as his dupes for these same purposes and that we, God's children, often become Satan's pawns or puppets. We often do his prompting even against our better judgment. Just look at the addictions available to us. Do we consider Lucifer to be the source of these addictions? When we yield to his temptations and influences, we retard our growth and the growth of those against whom we trespass, perhaps affecting their acceptance of the gospel. Thus, our actions may have an eternal consequence on the lives of others. The guilt and repercussions created by relenting to Lucifer's temptations may affect our spirituality for eternity. Each sin we commit has many tentacles not only affecting our lives but the lives of those around us. This is all part of Satan's plan to destroy us.

This war against mankind has been going on for over six thousand years. It started even before Eve partook of the forbidden fruit in the Garden of Eden. It began in the spirit world where Satan and his followers, by using their agency unwisely and non-righteously, failed in their attempt to entice us to rebel against God. He has since honed his skills as a battle-hardened force for evil and destruction, targeting everyone born into this world, especially the righteous. The only person strong enough to resist all of his temptations was our Savior Jesus Christ. The rest of us, more often than we like to admit, have been seduced by his promptings, urges, lies, deceits, and promises of pleasure, fun, wealth, power, excitement, and happiness to help in his rampage of chaos and destruction.

Satan has won a battle when he seduces us to do his bidding. Why are many of us so ready to respond to his deceits? Why are we enticed into believing that evil, in any form, is pleasurable or necessary and that Satan's pathways can bring happiness to us? Why do we often revel in bringing misery to others to get even? The answers to these questions are not simple.

Few of us would murder at the first provocation, but Satan can gradually take us down the long road of anger, evil, bias, and hate by getting us to surrender to his temptations and influences one at a time until finally, we are ready to kill, rape, or do any evil Satan has us believing is not only acceptable but needed. Satan will present us with the right incentive, motivation, and the right time to tempt us to do his bidding. It may be our tempers, greed, hatred, bias, or some other evil traits he has worked on until finally, we find it normal or appropriate, even necessary, to kill and do other evils. Satan would have us believe that this loss of control under the right conditions makes it acceptable and even desirable in some of our societies. Take a hard look at the television programs—at the evils depicted therein. There are murder, torture, mayhem, torment, and many other evils. Some of us become inured and believe that what we see on TV is normal, not evil, and even desirable. It's a small wonder that our younger generation adopts many of these same characteristics induced by societies that lack in teaching them the proper Christian ethics, morals, and discipline.

Gaming is another evil that wastes our time and is instrumental in creating an atmosphere that induces the player to kill, destroy, and create mayhem and destruction in many popular games in which we participate. Some people are very susceptible and suggestible to the material depicted in these games and will physically act on them, believing that there is no punishment involved knowing that it is all a game.

To be a winner in this war against Satan, we must constantly be on guard, studying and learning the methods and weapons he uses to destroy us. Then, we must learn to use the weapons God has given us to counter every move the adversary makes. We must always be alert to new thrusts and temptations so we can protect ourselves at all times and in all places always with the help of our Lord Jesus Christ.

The impact of Satan's influence on our lives must never be underestimated or he will win most of his battles. He has sworn and is committed to our physical, mental, emotional, and spiritual destruction. He doesn't worry about making a living, sleeping, taking vacations, families, or anything else, except devoting all of his time and energy to our downfall in both day and night. *Satan and his minions never rest and will never give up.*

Our only hope in winning this war is to heed God's council in the scriptures, our contemporary prophets, and spiritual leaders. We should also fast and pray for God's help, strength, and courage, then meditate and listen for his answer. We should accept and follow the law of repentance and baptism because it neutralizes the sins Satan has enticed us to commit. Also, we must extend love to those who are in the bondage of sin to help them regain the right status with our Savior. Satan would have us believe that repentance is futile—that there is no sin. This does not mean that we can deliberately sin with the intention of repenting and believe that all is well. To do this is really mocking God. The law of repentance is so important that Lucifer will devote much of his time convincing us that it is worthless, that our sins are too great to be forgiven, that there is no such thing as sin, and that it won't do any good anyway. Christ was only a teacher, not our redeemer. Lucifer plants these in or thoughts and many other fears, doubts, deceits, and lies into our hearts and minds and of all those who influence us in some way to confuse and lead us astray. He would have us believe that other channels are available for our salvation besides those provided by the gospel. He will also try to convince us that there is no life after death.

When we respond to Satan's influence and disobey God's laws and commandments, it is imperative that we repent as soon as possible before we die and none of us knows when that will be. If we die before we repent, we may not be forgiven.

Satan would have us believe that we are lost when we have committed some grievous sin—that there is no longer a need to strive for perfection. This is not so. Our Savior died for our sins, but they are only wiped clean when we repent, are baptized by proper authority, persevere in our efforts to progress, and become as perfect as possible and endure to the end. Repentance is a commandment from God, so we must all heed and obey this commandment, gain the courage, **be willing**, and act on this great necessity.

To prevent us from repenting, Lucifer will magnify and create fear within us. This may be fear of punishment, of retribution, fear that people will consider us less than how we present ourselves to the world, fear that others will look down on us, and fear of being rejected. He will use all of our fears and everything else at his disposal to keep us from seeing the proper authorities and repent. We may lack the courage to repent but with persistent prayers, determination, and the **willingness** to take the proper steps, we can return to our heavenly Father.

The only way to overcome these fears is by developing courage. We must pray for it; council with our friends for their sustaining strength and support; and council with our families and with our church leaders to whom we must go anyway to confess our more grievous sins. *What do we have to gain by being courageous—eternal life, forgiveness, joy, and happiness! What do we lose if we fail to develop and use our courage—we reap everlasting misery, pain, sorrow, and sickness! Christ will not forgive us if we do not seek repentance and baptism.* So, which is the best choice?

Through fasting, prayer, and perseverance, courage will most certainly come. These steps cannot be circumvented; they are necessary for our salvation and exaltation.

CHAPTER TEN

Satan's Power of Influences

How much power does Satan have over our lives? It's just as much as God and how much we allow! His power over us is so subtle that we don't or won't acknowledge it. For instance, take competition—in sports, we are in competition as individuals, teams, schools, counties, states, and countries to see who is the best. The rivalry between individuals and groups can be very intense at times, leading to bad feelings and violence. There is always a winner and a loser, creating an attitude of pride and disappointment. We are better than you, or we will beat you next time. Excelling in what we do in life is a good thing, but when we put pride and ill feelings into the equation, we see that Satan has had his influence in whatever the outcome is for each individual or team involved. Good sportsmanship and knowing that the opposing team or individual has done the very best they can may help some and may allay some of the pride and ill-feelings, but Satan has still injected his poison.

Competition is felt in many other aspects of our lives, such as business, work, sibling rivalry, etc., and the list goes on. The devil's influence will always be there to create contention, bias, havoc, and several other anger- and hate-based traits and attributes.

Striving for excellence and improving ourselves in righteous living and God-centered activities are what this life is all about, not competition. We are not in a competition to see who gets into the

Celestial kingdom. Righteous living is what will get us there, and not because we are better than anyone else. If we live our lives exerting our best efforts of which we are capable and help others to do the same, with the help of God, we can make it.

Satan can influence our thinking to devise ways to do evils of every kind to each other through wars and every other way possible. His temptations and influence have no bounds and no limits. No one is exempt from his temptations, lies, deceptions, promptings, and evils that lure us with promises of fun, excitement, power, and influence, which in the end, result in guilt and misery. This influence can be nullified by living the gospel.

Again, the devil never sleeps, never takes a vacation, and never gives up. He and his followers in both spiritual and physical are always active, plotting our demise 24/7.

The following are some of the many scriptures that may help us to overcome the evil promptings and influences of Satan:

> (1 Peter V 1–11) V 1 The elders which are among you I exhort, who am also an elder, and a witness of the sufferings of Christ, and also a partaker of the glory that shall be revealed;
>
> V 2 Feed the flock of God which is among you, taking the oversite *thereof,* not by constraint, but willingly; not for filthy lucre, but of a ready mind;
>
> V 3 Neither as being lords over *God's* heritage, but being ensamples to the flock.
>
> V 4 And when the chief Shepherd shall appear, ye shall receive a crown of glory that fadeth not away.
>
> V 5 Likewise, ye younger, submit yourselves unto the elder. Yea, all of you be subject one to another, and be clothed with humility: for God resisteth the proud, and giveth grace to the humble.
>
> V 6 Humble yourselves therefore under the mighty hand of God, that he may **exalt** you in due time: [emphasis added]
>
> V 7 Casting all your care upon him; for he careth for you.

V 8 Be sober, be vigilant; because the adversary, the devil, as a roaring lion, walketh about, seeking whom he may devour:

V 9 Whom resist, steadfast in the faith, knowing that the same afflictions are accomplished in your brethren that are in the world.

V 10 But the God of all grace, who hath called us unto his eternal glory by Christ Jesus, after that you have suffered awhile, make you perfect, stablish, strengthen, settle you.

V 11 To him be glory and dominion for ever and ever, amen.

(2 Ne. 2:11) For it needs be, that there is an opposition in all things.

(D&C. Sec. 58:26–31) *V-26 For behold, it is not meet that I should command in all things; for he that is compelled in all things, the same is a slothful and not a wise servant; wherefore he receiveth no reward.*

V-27 Verily I say, men should be anxiously engaged in a good cause, and do many things of their own free will, and bring to pass much righteousness;

V-28 For the power is in them, wherein they are agents unto themselves. And inasmuch as men do good, they shall in nowise lose their reward.

V-29 But he that doeth not anything until he is commanded, and receiveth a commandment with doubtful heart, and keepeth it with slothfulness, the same is damned.

V-30 Who am I that made man, saith the Lord, that will hold him guiltless that obeys not my commandments?

V-31 Who am I, saith the Lord, that have promised and not fulfilled? [emphasis added]

There is no facet of the human mind, body, spirit, or emotions that Satan will ignore in his pursuit of our destruction. There is no tool, instrument, method, activity, and no end to his use of individuals, groups, or alliances to accomplish his aims. He is so dedicated to his work that there is no end to his pursuits of bringing us pain, misery, and destruction. Absolutely nothing is sacred to him and he will never hesitate to change his methods and tactics. If one doesn't work, he will find another way to accomplish his miserable intentions. There is no single faction of the human race that he will omit in his obsessive actions to destroy them. Children and teenagers are among his favorite targets because of their vulnerability. God does try to protect them but their agency often puts them at risk because they like to try new things such as drugs, sex, and their drive to be recognized and to be accepted by their peers. Bullying is a favorite tool used on them, as is ostracization.

There are currently over seven billion human inhabitants of this earth. Every single one of these billions is being targeted, tempted, influenced, and induced to do some sort of evil every day of their lives. Some know what is going on and rejects these enticements while countless others due to weakness and the lure of fun, excitement, monetary gain, greed, power, and other temptations respond to Satan's promptings, making their life miserable through torture, maiming, and slaughtering other evils. The devil does all this not for gain or greed but for revenge, retaliation, payback, and retribution. This is an empty grudge against God and all those who didn't follow him in his rebellion. The devil's grudge can never be satisfied in or out of this world—it produces anger, hate, violence, contention, torture, pain, and death to human families which can never be gratified. So, Satan will continue this onslaught until the millennium when God puts a stop to it.

Below are some of the traits of both love and hate. The devil will either try to diminish and nullify love traits or expand and magnify the traits of hate and fear. He will try to diminish and nullify our emotions associated with the love traits, and he will amplify and magnify our emotions associated with hate and fear.

CHAPTER ELEVEN

Our Traits and Attributes

We live by the beliefs we have acquired in our lifetimes falling into these categories—those based on the unifying traits of love and those based on the disunifying, destructive traits of hate, anger, and fear. Many of these beliefs have been passed down to us from previous centuries and even millennia, and in our own lifetimes. Some of these beliefs come from the righteous powers of God and some from the powers of evil.

It is my opinion that our spirits during our pre-existence in the spiritual world accepted all teachings as truth. In this life, they probably also accept them as truth. Since Satan's efforts are to change truths by deceits and lies, we must then retrain our spirits that all is much different here than in the spirit world. Satan is rampant in the world, changing all truths into falsehoods which diminish or destroy our spiritual growth away from our goal of perfection. This presents the problem of our ability to discern truth from fiction and always presenting our spirits with nothing but the truth. If we had perfect discernment, there would be no problem but we don't, so our spirits receive what we feed them, and if this information is acted upon as a sin, then we must go through the process of repentance which nullifies the sin and teaches our spirits that it is sinful, and through repentance, it has been expunged. If we don't repent, we must carry the sin on into the spirit world (heaven) where we will go through a partial judgment to determine where we will be until the next and final judgment, heaven or the spirit prison, where we may receive further teaching and perhaps, ordinations.

Many of us believe that love is just an emotion, but in reality, love is much more complex. First, love only exists in the realm of the Father's kingdom as the base for the survival of all of his creations—the animation of all things physically, mentally, and emotionally including all life forms on land, air, and sea in this whole universe.

God's love cannot exist in Satan's realm.

Everything that does exist in God's creation is held in place by faith, which is an extension of love. All traits, characteristics, and attributes of the unifying elements are based in love as is all truth, harmony, and cohesiveness. In other words, nothing can exist without the power of love with all of its traits, characteristics, and attributes, many of which are shown below.

Satan's power exists in his control of all traits, characteristics, and attributes that are evil and negative. They, too, are shown below and the ability to either diminish or destroy the actions of our use of any of the traits of unity and love. Satan's aim is to destroy our desire to gain the kingdom of God through non-repentance, disobedience, and the destruction of our spiritual growth.

Spiritual growth is the only means whereby we can progress from grace to grace to the highest of God's kingdoms through repentance, obedience, accepting his many ordinances, and unconditionally embracing and rising above all of the trials and tribulations we undergo in this life.

Everything Satan does to debase and destroy us is centered on the spiritual growth process. His efforts never cease. His organization is almost endless in its sheer volume. His billions of fallen angels constitute his army, which is extremely efficient in bringing about our downfall. He never sleeps, rests, nor takes a vacation. He is never kind or loving and his patience never ends. He and his armies employ every device, stratagem, and scheme at his command to destroy our spiritual growth. Become aware of the divergent methods, lies, deceits, and the attractive promises which entice us away from our spiritual growth path to the Celestial kingdom. Satan is so devious that without God, we don't have a chance.

To counter these satanic forces of destruction is by following God's laws and commandments, especially those pertaining to love.

We live by the beliefs and belief systems we have acquired in our lifetimes. They come to us in many forms and in many ways. Some come to us from the traditions of our families, states, countries, clans, etc. There are religious beliefs that have come to us millennia ago. Satan has changed true beliefs down through the ages by influencing those who were receptive to change into beliefs that do not resemble the original meaning.

How can we know which changes have been made by Satan's influences on the beliefs we consider to be true? The answer to this question is another question! Will this belief give me the answers to obtain spiritual growth to bring me back to our heavenly Father? Satan will give us many false methods that seem truthful or at least acceptable to hinder us back to the Father. The right answers will come **by** searching, fasting, praying, and obeying God's laws and commandments and by reading and studying all of the available scriptures. Always ask this one question! Will this answer get me into God's kingdom through spiritual growth?

Truth stands alone to that which exists in all events, happenings, all lives, and in fact, anything and everything that we can hear, see, taste, feel, smell, or experience. However, Satan can alter our memories and increase or decrease the sensations involved with all of the above. There is no time limit, past, present, or future that he will use to lie and deceive us.

Truth cannot be changed from its purity. It is what it is but our perception of almost anything can and will be altered by Satan. It is one of the major targets he uses to change, deceive, and confuse us.

Satan will deceive us, lie to us, change the good to look evil, and make evil look good in appearance. His methods are so subtle that it becomes easy for us to change our minds to his viewpoints. His methods are so varied that his changes are very difficult to detect, and many of us fall for his snare and deceits so we inadvertently become his dupes doing his bidding. Eventually, if we are not aware, we become part of his army fighting against humanity.

Truth is beautiful, truth is essential, and we cannot grow spiritually without it. We should all become truth-seekers for if not, we could become one of Satan's slaves!

Below, I have selected a few of the unifying traits of love and the disunifying traits of hate.

UNIFYING TRAITS AND ATTRIBUTES OF LOVE

These are some of approximately five hundred traits of which Satan uses to diminish their effectiveness through his promptings and influences.

To the best of our abilities and efforts, the perfection and magnification of the following traits, attributes, and characteristics are in my opinion, part of what our Lord and Savior expects of us in this life. Peace and contentment will surely follow as we apply our energies to this endeavor. If we allow, Satan will diminish and weaken each of these traits of love, unity, and righteousness as we use them in our daily lives:

Activity, ambition, appreciation, awareness, benevolence, charity, cleanliness, commitment, compassion, confidence, consistency, courage, creativity, dedication, discernment, durability, empathy, equality, faith, forgiveness, friendliness, gentleness, godliness, helpfulness, honesty, honor, hope, humility, humor, industry, inquisitiveness, integrity, intention, justice, kindness, knowledge, love, meekness, mercy, meditation, modesty, morality, motivation, obedience, organization, patience, persistence, preparedness, promptness, purity, repentance, resilience, resolution, responsibility, reverence, righteousness, sacrifice, discipline, self-esteem, self-reliance, sensitivity, serenity, sharing, spirituality, stability, steadfastness, studious, success, surrendering, tact, temperance, thoughtfulness, trust, virtue, and watchfulness.

Each of the above traits, characteristics, and attributes are love and righteousness oriented. They and all others falling in the same category are those which we need to *perfect* on our journey through this life and during the millennium; the Celestial kingdom as our goal. These and all the others not shown here that fall into this category are those which, in my opinion, are ordained of God and that when perfected in their entirety, makes us one hundred percent spiritually clean and pure in his eyes.

The following traits, characteristics, and attributes are based on fear, hate, evil, and unrighteousness. The ones mentioned here, plus all the others not identified in this work, must all be controlled or expunged from all of our ***thoughts and actions***. These are evil by nature and cannot be present as part of our lives when we are judged by Christ at the end of the millennium. It is my opinion that our possession or use of any of these fear and hate-based elements when we are judged will find us spiritually unclean and that consequently, we cannot live in the presence of the Deity and those who have become completely clean every whit.

UNRIGHTEOUS, DESTRUCTIVE, DIVISIVE, TRAITS OF HATE AND FEAR

These are some of the approximately five hundred traits and characteristics which Satan and his hoards use to magnify and amplify their evil influences to enhance their desire or aim to destroy us. For instance, he may amplify anger into wrath, wrath into rage, rage into fury, and any of which causing a complete breakdown of our control. The results could lead us down to destruction.

To the best of our abilities and efforts, the purging, diminishing, and eliminating the use of the following attributes, characteristics, and traits are, in my opinion, what our Lord and Savior expects of us in this life and during the millennium. Failure to give our best efforts in rejecting and expunging them will surely fail to produce the expected results. These elements are some of the many tools Satan uses to torture and destroy us. He will magnify and expand each of these traits as we employ them in our everyday lives:

Anger, arguments, apathy, avarice, bias, blindness, callousness, cheating, contempt, contention, controlling, cowardice, cruelty, devilishness, dishonesty, disloyalty,

disobedient, disorderly, disorganized, disdainful, destructive, doubt, dread, dueling, enslavement, envy, evil-mindedness, yielding, gossip, greed, grudges, hostility, hardheartedness, hate, intolerance, irreverence, irresponsible, insincere, jealousy, laziness, lying, lust, malevolence, malicious, mean, merciless, negative, uncommitted, uncaring, non-creative, non-discerning, non-empathetic, non-dependence, undisciplined, non-meditative, non-motivated, non-persistent, non-repentant, non-seeking, polluting, non-prayerful, obnoxious, opinionated, obsessive, oppressive, obstinate, otiose, prejudice, pride, procrastination, sad, selfish, self-centered, revenge, sloppy, slothful, tactless, thankless, thoughtless, unchaste, non-enduring, unforgiving, unlawful, non-prayerful, unprepared, unrighteous, unskilled, unsuccessful, unsure, unteachable, untrustworthy, non-virtuous, vacillation, and weakness.

Here is one of many examples Satan uses to make it appear like sinning is normal and acceptable—the plots of many movies and programs are designed to sway us to believe that violence and killing are normal and acceptable under the influence of anger, hate, and bias-oriented disunifying traits and attributes.

In using these evil traits, Satan is more dedicated to getting us under his control to do his bidding than to destroy us in death.

These are the last days; the time is ready; and the field is becoming ripe for the heavenly Father to search the field and select those who have been obedient from those who have procrastinated the day of their repentance, and haven't believed or cared what God has in store for the repentant and righteous among us.

JUST HOW FAR WILL GOD ALLOW LUCIFER TO GO IN HIS EFFORTS TO DESTROY MANKIND? *IT IS ONLY AS FAR AS WE AND GOD ALLOW. GOD'S INTERVENTION TO BALANCE THE SCALES AND PREVENT LUCIFER'S HOARDS FROM DESTROYING OUR AGENCY IS ABSOLUTELY NECESSARY TO PRESERVE OUR RIGHT TO CHOOSE, AND SO WE MUST REPENT, PRAY FOR THE COURAGE AND STRENGTH TO SEEK GOD'S GUIDANCE, AND INTERCEDE FOR US, OR WE WON'T MAKE IT.*

I do a great disservice to God in trying to describe his great love for us, and for the great power he wields in our favor, hopefully, to keep us on the right track to the Celestial kingdom if we want it enough and allow it.

God does not look at the outside of man as we do to determine our worth, but only at the inside where our hearts and minds reside. This not only applies to the congregations of his church here on the earth but everywhere that the good and noble reside or exist. He is here for all of us to guide and direct us into and along the path he has chosen for us if we will but listen, heed his callings and promptings, and follow his path.

We can say that we love him, but until we can feel the awesomeness, the magnitude, and the height, breadth, and depth of God's love, and understand that everything he does is because of that great love, we will only be uttering the words.

I believe we all made a contract etched in our hearts and minds before we came to earth to do the best of which we are capable and to follow Christ and his teachings. How well has each of us fulfilled that contract? His love for each and every one of us is eternal. We must allow him to help us complete that contract and stay on the path back to him.

There is a law irrevocably decreed in heaven before the foundations of the world upon which all blessings are predicated and when any blessing is received of God. It is by obedience to that law upon which it is predicated.

(D & C 130:20–21) When we don't obtain a blessing we have prayed for, we need to look inward and examine whether we have obeyed the law or laws required to receive it. If we have, again we need to look inward to see if we deserve it. God knows what is best for us and he may withhold a blessing if it is not in our best interest.

The law of love is based on the following commandments in Matt. 22:36–40:

> (A Pharisee lawyer asked Jesus)
> V 36 Master, what is the great commandment in the law?

> V 37 Jesus said unto him, thou shalt love the Lord thy God with all thy heart, and with all thy soul, and with all thy mind.
>
> V 38 This is the first and great commandment.
>
> V 39 And the second is like unto it, thou shalt love thy neighbor as thyself.
>
> V 40 On these two commandments hang all the law and the prophets.

The most important of these two commandments is to love the Lord thy God with all thy heart and with all thy soul and with all thy mind.

So how do we love our Lord God? If our love for God and for others does not meet his requirements, we probably won't receive the requested blessing.

The Lord said if you love me, keep my commandments (D & C 59:5-6—If thou lovest me thou shalt serve me and keep all my commandments). Does it mean only keeping the commandments we want to at any given time? Or does it mean keeping his commandments only when we feel like it?

What would Satan have us do?

If we don't obey one of his commandments, does that mean we don't love the Lord or that there is no longer any hope for us?

It is very easy to get bogged down with questions like those above. To love the Lord unconditionally means that we love him with all our hearts, minds, strength, and soul no matter what he does. No one can ever know all of the reasons why God does what he does or doesn't do, or what we think he should do. Even if he told us all the reasons, we probably couldn't comprehend it all, because we don't have the background, wisdom, knowledge, or intelligence. God's knowledge, wisdom, intelligence, power, and glory are so far above ours that to question him on any issue is only showing how unwise and foolish we are.

These last days will be filled with questions about God, from the ignorant who have no clue why we are here, or what God has in store for those who love and obey him. The tares and wheat are being separated right now. There are those who know this, and are preparing for Christ's second coming with expectation, appreciation, and love for him, giving our best efforts to obey all his commandments all of the time and also accepting all his actions and judgments without question. There will be those who say Christ isn't coming because the time is past when he should have been here. There will be thousands of excuses for doing evil things because he isn't here yet. Please don't get bogged down with all these excuses. Christ will get here when his Father tells him it is time. Satan will do his best to interfere with every evil at his disposal to sidetrack us from remaining true to his laws and commandments.

CHAPTER TWELVE

Satan's Control

There is no facet of humankind that Satan has not influenced or controlled with his lies, deceits, influences, promptings, temptations, and with our destruction as his goal.

In these last days, it will be difficult for us to discern good from evil. Some will believe that evil is good and that good is evil. If we look around, we can see this happening already. This is the last time Satan will have to destroy or enslave us. It is my opinion that his efforts will now be greater than at any time in the earth's history. Satan will pull out all of the stops in his last-ditch efforts to attain his goal of making slaves to those who would rather follow him than Christ and destroying all that is good and righteous. The carnage and devastation we will be subjected to will turn our hearts and minds to say, "Why would God allow such heinous and terrible things to happen to the human race?"

This and many other questions will be asked before the end just like before the second coming. Don't believe the things Satan whispers to us—that there is no God, no Christ, no sin, no repentance, no spirit, or that when this life is over, there is nothing so it matters not what we do while here on earth. It all depends on what we believe we can get away with. These and many other lies and deceits will be hurled our way to take us away from our Savior who will be there to help us repent and keep us on the track to his kingdom if we will but listen to his still small voice. The slings and arrows hurled at us will make our hearts tell us that this is the end. We can know the truth of all things if we do listen to that still small voice of the Holy Ghost. He cannot and will not deceive or lie to us. It is so very important that we have unconditional love for God, Jesus Christ, and the Holy Ghost and know that these are the days when the wheat is being separated from the tares. In other words, we are being judged and selected for whichever power we desire to follow—Christ's or Satan's. We will be whatever we have chosen to be—the wheat or the tares. We will either be burned with the tares or be caught up to meet our Savior. The choice is definitely ours to make. There are two very important absolutes that will definitely take place—first, we will all die; second, we will all be judged not only for what we have done and not repented of but for what we have become. These two things are inevitable and should help us determine which path we take, Christ's or Satan's. No one is exempt from these two absolutes. It doesn't matter what we believe or don't believe—these two events will happen.

Have we ever considered the reasons why we often select Satan's path rather than the plan of salvation? The answer is really very simple—it is much harder to follow Christ's plan than Satan's. His plan requires little or no effort while God's plan requires study, thankfulness, much prayer, supplication, and obedience to his laws and commandments, and of course our love for God, Jesus Christ, and our neighbors. What is the end result for each path? God's path, if followed as required, brings to us joy and happiness and living again with him for eternity. Following Satan's path brings us only sadness, misery, guilt, unhappiness, and the destruction of our minds, bodies, and spirits, resulting in an eternity of suffering of such an intensity that we at this time cannot begin to comprehend. Looking at the choices we have, the selection seems easy to make. Of course, there are many mansions in the three kingdoms of God waiting for us, which means that there are many judgments for each kingdom. Being cast into outer darkness with Satan is the most severe of the judgments and brings the most intense suffering for eternity—this is not a kingdom of God!

When Satan's carnage and destruction are at their peak and he has sealed his own, God will take those who remain true to him in the clouds to be with him as the earth burns in the cleansing promised by the prophets of old and new. The wheat is now being separated from the tares which will be burned with the cleansing. After Satan has sealed his own, there will be earthquakes, famines, great whirlwinds, and seas roaring over their bounds. The earth will reel to and fro like a drunken man [this all comes from the scriptures]. The calamities will be so great that men's hearts will fail them. Stars will fall from the heavens. Mountains and valleys will disappear and the whole earth will become unrecognizable. What is left will be the terrestrial earth ready for the habitation of those who have been true to the Savior's teachings, obedient to his commandments, and who have lived the law of love and repentance. To understand these happenings, read the book of Daniel, Revelations, Isaiah, Ezekiel, The Doctrine and Covenants, The Book of Mormon, and many other scriptures.

Satan's war isn't over yet. At the end of the millennium, he will be loosed for a brief period, to tempt those who haven't been subjected to his deceits and lies, then comes the final judgment which will determine what God has in store for each of us through the eternities.

Because the devil rebelled against God, he was cast out of heaven and exiled down to earth with a third of the hosts of heaven who had also rebelled.

Satan's plan was to save each and every one of God's children, but he wanted the glory to be his. Also, he would take away from man the power to choose, his agency, which would leave man without a means of returning back to the Father [all of the above information comes from the Holy Scriptures; a retranslation of the Holy Bible, King James Version by the Prophet Joseph Smith Jr.].

Let us now view some of the evils that he has produced down through the ages.

The first recorded temptation of Satan was when he lured Eve into partaking of the fruit of the knowledge of good and evil. He then tempted Eve again by getting her to tempt Adam who also partook of the fruit. From then until the flood, it was one chaotic acceptance of temptation after another until the whole world was in chaos and disarray and had to be cleansed by water (the earth's baptism).

Eight souls were saved who were righteous enough to start the procreation of the human race over again. From the flood until the coming of Christ to the Jews and from then until now, satanic evil has continued to expand into every aspect of our lives. Now the earth is again reaching the point where it needs to be cleansed and this time, by fire. The righteous living and dead will then be caught up in the clouds to meet our Savior as he comes to begin the thousand years of his millennial reign. Satan will then be bound and unable to tempt man for a thousand years; after which time, he will be loosed for a brief period to entice those who had not yet been tempted.

Since the beginning of life on earth, there have been literally *billions* of the human family who have been tempted, lured, and persuaded to follow Satan's path to destruction. He has us believing that his is the only way, and so many of us have blindly followed his enticing and consequently are now under his control. The only way back to the Deity is through repentance, which Satan would have us believe is unnecessary, making us believe that our sins are too great to be forgiven or that we don't need it to be saved. There are many hundreds of ways that Satan uses to blind our minds. His lies are pervasive and seemingly have no end and must be very believable because so many of us do believe his deceptions. The only hope we have is in God's plan of salvation and exaltation instituted by him to bring us all back home to him if we repent.

None of us need to be frightened at the prospects that Lucifer has the upper hand, and that by and large, we are all doomed. Don't ever believe such lies. Turning back to God may be hard but it is essential. He has never said it would be easy; just that it is absolutely necessary. Doing what is right may never be easy or popular. What is essential is that we identify the path, overcome, and conquer all adversities and rise above and repent of them all with the help of God, Jesus Christ, and the Holy Ghost.

Here are some final words on what I believe God would like our behavior to become in this life.

Believing that we can just coast through this life and all will be well if we don't commit any gross sin is another guise Satan uses to confuse us. In the end, our false beliefs may condemn us. Satan uses our false beliefs and our non-truthful traditions which have plagued us through the centuries being passed on from family to family so that we finally become so entrenched with them that it is extremely difficult to dislodge. The Holy Ghost is the purveyor of all truth and will touch the minds and hearts of those who search. Our missionaries are the ones God has chosen to encourage the world to search for the truth.

To help overcome the destructive traits, characteristics, and attributes advocated by Satan, I am including many prayer affirmations that may help to eliminate any or all of these evils used by Lucifer and his minions. A prayer affirmation may be used for any of these unwanted traits and with a slight modification, used to expand and magnify all of the characteristics, traits, and attributes of love and unity. If we are not sincere and don't really desire the outcome of the affirmations listed in this work, there is no use trying. I believe that God would have us all be dead serious and desire the help these affirmations can give to us and help them to be effective. Here is one of the prayer affirmations:

Father in heaven, with the wonderful and eternal help from thee and thy son, Jesus Christ, and the Holy Ghost, to whom I am most thankful, and with their approval, I now ask thee to please open my mind, heart, and spirit to accept thy great healing powers which will help me expunge and release all of my doubts that prevent me from using and magnifying my faith. This powerful affirmation will now penetrate to the very depths of my mind, body, and spirit, in the sacred name of Jesus Christ, amen [Repeat four times daily aloud, with meaning and commitment for one month, then choose another affirmation, from those which follow later, with this same pattern].

Defusing or diminishing any righteous event is the work and promptings of Satan whom we should never heed.

The following is one example of Satan at work using his army of humans to do his will in their rampage of destruction.

Every incident of the initiation of wars, insurrections, riots, terrorist activities, etc. has their beginnings with the devil who gains control of men and women through promises of wealth, power, and other goodies. These (leaders) attain a following by enlisting others with the promise of power and high positions in the organization he is creating whom Satan convinces that it is for the good of mankind. There are always those under Satan's control willing to follow any despotic leader who fancies himself as a reformer or rebuilder of nations under socialism, communism, fascism, or some other evil forms of government. As this organization gains strength through numerical growth by promises many of which are never fulfilled, they infiltrate governments and any other organization that is susceptible to their evil plans—Satan and his minions are at work on every person involved in this evil undertaking. We can see this plan at work in our own government as one faction tries by every means possible to undermine and make invalid our legally elected president through a vast majority of our electorate.

This organization was well on its way to change this country into a socialistic and then communistic form of government until the electorate changed the direction of their takeover. Without any consideration for the electorate, they have gone ahead with their evil plans to make invalid the legally seated president. If they succeed in their evil undertaking, this country will go downhill at a very rapid pace.

It doesn't take much imagination to see what could happen if we as a nation sit back on our laurels and let it happen. Were it to happen, the new government in charge would try to dislodge our constitution and have a cleansing like the communist countries, which have resulted in the elimination of vast portions of our world's population to the extent of twenty to thirty million and more just like in the Soviet Union, China, and other communist countries. What do Satan and his minions get as a reward for instigating these terrible events? It is my belief that they gain those who love the suffering of mankind, just like we love to see our acquaintances happy and forgiving.

Many leaders of our nations around the world are subject to this same theme, probably with many variations. It's amazing to me how these leaders make decisions that seem halfway innocent at the time but when added upon with other seemingly innocent decisions, which we as the world's population don't understand, many of us seem to care less how it will affect us in the future. Those who have given their lives over to Satan will have to pay for their iniquities in the future unless they repent. It is my opinion that most world leaders and governments have relinquished their beliefs on Christianity and righteousness and don't believe that they will ever be responsible for their evil actions.

There is a plethora of other subterfuges, lies, and deceits used by Satan and his minions which most of us won't accept as coming from his influences. We may be held responsible for not knowing God's word because the information is here in the scriptures for us to read, study, accept, or reject. Satan will use everything at his disposal to keep us from studying and accepting the plan of salvation and exaltation. It is a long, hard road toward accepting the ordinance of baptism, which is necessary to get right with our heavenly Father, and very few will make the effort to receive and accept his teachings.

If you really want to see Lucifer at work, watch the news and almost every other program, movie, or newspaper. Also, watch our governments at work; many seem not to care that Satan is at work among them and uses many of us to destroy our great nations. Is reading and studying Christianity too much to do? Are the pressures from both social and governmental entities too much to overcome? Believe me, it is well worth the effort!

As I have written this expose, I find that no matter where I look, I see the devil's forces at work. The television's news programs are especially loaded with the effects of his fiendish influences. There is no place to hide to avoid his evil designs. If I were to hide in the deepest cave, I would find that he had followed me there. I can't even hide from myself, and as I look inward, I see the effects of Satan's influences on my thinking and actions on which ***I will be judged if I do not repent***. Everywhere I look, I see the devastation he has created and is continuing to create. There is no end to his evils and there wouldn't be until Christ comes to begin his millennial reign. The very sad part of this scenario is that all of the terrible, evil, wicked, sinful, malevolent, foul, and malicious things that have happened and are happening now have been perpetrated by humans under the influence of Satan and his hoards.

I now look at the world much differently than before I began this work. As I look at the occurrences of the evils surrounding me, I find myself evaluating every experience, every thought, every movie, etc., to determine what influences Satan has had on me. As I view things, I now look inward to see if I'm guilty of entertaining Satan's influence in my life. It has really made a difference in that I am now more able to discern the evils he is inflicting on us, God's children. What a blessing this has been for me!

What can we do before our Savior comes? That is an easy question to answer—bring God and Christ back into our lives and see what he is doing all around us! He is in complete control of the weather, the farmlands, the earthquakes, volcanoes, and famines—in fact, every facet of our lives around the world. If we would just stop, listen, and ask ourselves why he is bringing these calamities on earth at this time, we would know that his second coming is nearing. If we could just recognize that God is trying to get our attention and admit that it is, indeed, him to whom we should turn and repent as individuals, nations, organizations, churches, etc. If we as a nation would turn back to God and be hundred percent active Christians, we would once again be enormously blessed, and Satan would have little influence over us. This is so simple to do. Perhaps, we may have gone too far to be redeemed as a nation. With God's help, nothing is impossible. However, it will take a massive movement of the members of every church, organization, and society in every country in the world to make it happen. **Let's just do what is necessary in the eyes of God!**

One more thought—Satan controls to a large extent the thinking of many of our politicians, the gaming moguls, news media, movies, comedians, clubs, organizations, etc., who try to control our thinking or influence our minds that evil activities and thinking are great fun, which leads to actions related to

that thinking. If we let God's thinking through the Holy Ghost affect our thoughts which lead to righteous actions, it will bring us closer to the perfection commanded of us. If we learn the difference between the Holy Ghost's promptings and Satan's influences and choose God's way, we will be in alignment and in harmony with his desires for us.

I believe the greatest power in the universe is love. God is love. The greatest commandment under the law is in Matthew 22:37–40:

> V 37 Jesus said unto him, thou shalt love the Lord thy God with all thy heart, and with all thy soul, and with all thy mind.
> V 38 This is the first and great commandment.
> V 39 and the second is like unto it, thou shalt love thy neighbor as thyself.
> V 40 On these two commandments hang all the law and the prophets.

In my opinion, love is the greatest power in the universe from which all unifying traits, attributes, and characteristics spring. God is love, and the greatest commandment under the law is to love God as he loves us unconditionally. All of God's family should develop this unconditional love for him and for all of his children. To love God unconditionally means that we accept and obey all of his laws, commandments, and every action and everything he does, even that which brings every calamity known to man onto this earth. It is not our right or privilege to question or judge what he does. His knowledge, wisdom, intelligence, power, and glory are so far above our comprehension that only the grossly uninformed would question any of his actions. Know this that God's every action has a purpose and that it is for our growth towards the perfection commanded by him.

CHAPTER THIRTEEN

Our Beliefs and Belief Systems

Beliefs and belief systems are among the most effective tools (weapons) in Satan's arsenal. Also, they are among the greatest weapons God and his followers use to counter the forces of evil.

We live by the beliefs and belief systems we have acquired in our lifetimes. Some are based on righteous truths, while others are based on falsehoods, lies, and deceits. We attain them from early childhood and on through adulthood. Many are passed down from generation to generation for hundreds and even for thousands of years. The longer we employ and conform to them without seeking the truth or falsehood of those beliefs, the deeper the roots and the more difficult they become to remove or change. Change beliefs and we are changed for the better or the worst, for good or evil. Some beliefs even start wars while others make it possible for people to torture, maim, betray, kill, and produce many other evil actions against humanity.

Beliefs also allow us to prevent these evils and can make it impossible for them to happen, utilizing the power of love. Beware of those beliefs not founded in truth and love. For many, this may be a difficult thing to do since many beliefs are handed down from generation to generation, and we are comfortable with the anger, hate, and bias, etc. with which we are so very familiar.

All that we respond to and are willing to accept which come from Lucifer and the influence he has on those who distress us and those influences coming from the Holy Ghost determines where we will be in the eternities, as shown below.

If we can only abide by the laws governing the Telestial glory (kingdom or world), then that is where we will be the happiest.

> (1 Corinthians 15:41) V 41 There is one glory of the sun, another glory of the moon and another glory of the stars: for one star differeth from another star in glory.
>
> (D & C 88: 22 –24) V 22 For he who is not able to abide the law of a celestial kingdom cannot abide a celestial glory.
>
> V 23 And he who cannot abide the law of a terrestrial kingdom cannot abide a terrestrial glory.
>
> V 24 And he who cannot abide the law of a telestial kingdom cannot abide a telestial glory; therefore he is not meet for a kingdom of glory. Therefore he must abide a kingdom, which is not a kingdom of glory.
>
> V 31 And they who are quickened by a portion of the telestial glory shall then receive of the same, even a fullness.

My point is that Satan has set up many hundreds or even thousands of situations, conditions, and events which may have been introduced many years, even centuries and millennia ago, putting in place beliefs, belief systems, traditions, and many other situations that create havoc in our present-day existence. These events range from religious beliefs to racial, monetary, intelligence, country against country, state against state, men against women, women against men, etc. The most puzzling thing is that humanity buys into Satan's toying with our minds, not realizing that these events were set in motion many years ago. His aim is to bring as many of us as possible under his control to do his bidding and just about anything else we could name to cause our destruction, pain misery, etc.

While I was watching a movie the other day, it came to me that Satan had his influence in creating the plot for the movie, which was to make it acceptable for us to use hate and anger, to accept violence and even death, and to justify our actions that result from using these traits.

Traditions are another of Satan's major tools which have been meticulously generated many times, hundreds, or even thousands of years ago in families, counties, states, countries, religions, organizations, etc. to pit one faction against another, thinking that one is better, more righteous, smarter, etc. than the others. These traditions are very difficult to dislodge as they have been in use for so long. More recently, these traditions have been created between our sports, industries, and many other institutions which create antagonisms, violence, and even death.

Traditions can be either good or evil and many times, it is difficult to tell the difference of one from the other, especially when it comes to our religious beliefs. Wars are being, and have been, fought over these beliefs and traditions. Satan has organized them so they are difficult to overcome and dislodge.

God's love for us and our love for each other are some of the tools I have found that can break down these barriers and bring us together as children of God. Other tools that are effective are tolerance, kindness, and all the other unifying traits. Gaining knowledge of people's traditions helps us understand and discern the differences.

It would take thousands of volumes to name all of the controls Satan has over the human race—there are human trafficking, sexual enslavement, human bondage, all types of torture, mental illness, and emotional problems. You could go on and on and barely touch the influences and horrors brought on us by Satan and his masses of evil spirits, and those of us who heed and execute his evil designs for the human race.

If the world would just identify the destructive beliefs that bring us into subjection to Satan's powers, and conquer, rise above, and expunge them from our lives, what a different world this could be.

Just contemplating the three kingdoms of glory mentioned above, one of which we will probably inherit, should give us all the desire to study Satan's power and the war machines he is using against us, second by second, minute by minute every day to destroy and bring pain to us and others. If we had the courage and prayed for the willingness and courage to change, we could set our sights on the attainment of the Celestial kingdom and live with God and Christ whose help we need to accomplish it.

The following prayer affirmations allow the reader to have other weapons based in love with which we can counter the devastating weapons of hate and disunity used by Satan and his followers, both alive, and in the spiritual realm. Beliefs and the unwillingness to change puts us at a disadvantage unless we rely on our Father in heaven to show us the way to victory.

Satan has already sealed many of the living and the dead to his army, and also those people who will be relegated to the lessor of God's three kingdoms of glory. What we need is the ***courage and willingness*** to put forth the effort needed to examine our beliefs, belief systems, and traditions; gain the knowledge, wisdom, and intelligence to go against popular opinions and dogmas accepted by the world as a whole; and with prayer and sincere supplication, approach our Lord for his help in making the decisions and necessary changes to our lifestyles which are absolutely necessary to regain his presence.

Here are some of the scriptures that inform us of the powers of Satan and his followers. This first one comes from the Book of Mormon, 2 Nephi chapter 23 starting with verse 6 and from Isaiah chapter 13:

> V 6 Howl ye, for the day of the Lord is at hand; it shall come as a destruction from the Almighty,
>
> V 7 Therefore shall all hands be faint, every man's heart shall melt;
>
> V 8 And they shall be afraid; pangs and sorrows shall take hold of them; they shall be amazed one at another; their faces shall be as flames.
>
> V 9 Behold, the day of the Lord cometh, cruel both with wrath and fierce anger, to lay the land desolate; and he shall destroy the sinners thereof out of it.
>
> V 10 For the stars of heaven and the constellations thereof shall not give their light; the sun shall be darkened

in her going forth, and the moon shall not cause her light to shine.

V 11 And I will punish the world for evil, and the wicked for their iniquity; I will cause the arrogancy of the proud to cease and will lay down the haughtiness of the terrible.

V 12 I will make a man more precious than fine gold; even a man than the golden wedge of Ophir.

V 13 Therefore, I will shake the heavens, and the earth hall remove out of her place, in the wrath of the Lord of of hosts, and in the day of his fierce anger.

V 14 And it shall be as the chased roe, and as a sheep that no man taketh up; and they shall every man turn to his own people and flee every one into his own land.

V 15 Every one that is proud shall be thrust through; yea, and every one that is joined to the wicked shall fall by the sword.

V 16 Their children also shall be dashed to pieces before their eyes; their houses shall be spoiled and their wives ravished.

V 17 Behold, I will stir up the Medes against them, which shall not regard silver and gold, nor shall they delight in it.

V 18 Their bows shall also dash the young men to pieces, and they shall have no pity on the fruit of the womb; their eyes shall not spare children.

V 19 And Babylon, the glory of kingdoms, the beauty of the Chaldees' shall be as when God overthrew Sodom and Gomorrah.

V 20 It shall never be inhabited, neither shall it be dwelt in from generation to generation: neither shall the Arabian pitch tent there; neither shall the shepherds make their fold there.

V 21 But wild beasts of the desert shall lie there; and their houses shall be full of doleful creatures; and owls shall dwell there, and satyrs shall dance there.

V 22 And the wild beasts of the islands shall cry in their desolate houses, and dragons in their pleasant palaces; and her time is near to come, and her day shall

> not be prolonged. For I will destroy her speedily; yea, for I will be merciful unto my people, but the wicked shall perish.

The above scriptures present us with an excellent view of what's coming in the near future. It is my opinion that these are the last days and Satan will be hard at work more so than at any other time in the history of this world. His efforts will exceed all his other attempts to destroy us. Following God's plan is our only hope.

The following is one of the many scenarios Satan and his minions use to bring us under his control—firstly, they select a target, creates anger, then hate within the target for someone, something, or some faction for some inconsequential event, etc.; secondly, they magnify, nourish, and expand the bias, anger, and hate—he then and encourages their target to act out some form of evil which hurts or may even destroy their victims; thirdly, Satan gives the target excuses for the action and encourages retaliation and retribution if we allow. We can see this scenario being played out every day in every facet of our daily lives. We must all be aware of this scenario and not fall into its trap.

This is another scenario that Satan uses to weaken our attempts to use any of the righteous traits and characteristics to help someone. As an example, I have used love to demonstrate that of which Satan is capable. First, Satan identifies his target who is demonstrating love for someone by helping them in some way. He then attempts to diminish, disavow, and lessen its effectiveness and even render it ineffective when the target allows.

Always be aware of what Satan tries to do to us. There are many diverse affirmations which are effective to a degree, but most of them omit using the powers of God to help them overcome the many obstacles and gain perfection of which he has commanded. Listed below are two styles of prayer affirmations I have used which are very effective and do include the Deity.

Using your own format is acceptable, but please include God and his son, which will strengthen their effectiveness. Here are some that I have found to be very effective.

The following formats have proven to be very successful and will be used on both the uniting and the separating traits, attributes, and characteristics:

HEAVENLY FATHER, WITH THE AID OF JESUS CHRIST AND THE HOLY GHOST, PLEASE HELP ME RECOGNIZE THAT MY **ANGER** PROBLEM IS MY RESPONSIBILITY TO CHOOSE BETWEEN THE HOLY GHOST AND THE SATANIC FORCES OF EVIL. MY ACQUIRING IT ORIGINATED IN MY ACCEPTING THE VALUE OF **ANGER** TO GET MY WAY AND TO GET POWER OVER OTHERS. I HAVE LEARNED THIS TRAIT BY WATCHING MY PARENTS, SIBLINGS, RELATIVES, MOVIES, TELEVISION, AND MANY OTHER SOURCES, AND BY HELPING THEM WIN ARGUMENTS, EXERT POWER, AND OTHER UNWELCOME ACTIVITIES. I KNOW THAT I CHOSE AND AM STILL, FREQUENTLY, CHOOSING THE PROMPTINGS OF SATAN INSTEAD OF THE HOLY GHOST WHEN I EXPRESS MY **ANGER**. I NOW REALIZE THAT **ANGER** HAS BECOME SO ENTRENCHED IN MY PERSONALITY THAT IT HAS BECOME AN AUTOMATIC RESPONSE TO MANY STIMULI—LEARNED DURING MY ENTIRE LIFE. PLEASE HELP ME TO EXPUNGE IT FROM EVERYDAY USAGE WHICH I NOW GLADLY WELCOME. MAKE ME EVER AWARE OF THE NEED TO ELIMINATE MY USAGE OF ANGER TO SOLVE ANY PROBLEM THAT ARISES. HELP ME USE LOVE AND CARE INSTEAD. THIS AFFIRMATION WILL NOW PENETRATE TO THE VERY DEPTHS OF MY MIND, BODY, AND SPIRIT IN THE HOLY NAME OF JESUS CHRIST, AMEN.

I AM NOW CALLING ON THE INFINITE POWER AND ETERNAL HELP OF GOD, JESUS CHRIST, THE HOLY GHOST, AND WITH ABSOLUTE FAITH, GRATITUDE, AND UNCONDITIONAL LOVE FOR THEM AND WITH THEIR APPROVAL, I BELIEVE I DESERVE TO USE MY UNWAVERING DESIRE TO OVERCOME, CONQUER, AND RISE ABOVE THE DIFFICULTIES AND AFFLICTIONS

THAT PREVENT ME FROM USING MY **FAITH** TO PERFECT MY RIGHTEOUS ENDEAVORS. I WILL NOW DEFINITELY FORGIVE MYSELF FOR NOT DESERVING THIS SACRED BLESSING. THIS IS MY COMMITMENT FROM THIS MOMENT ON AND FOREVER. I AM NOW DETERMINED TO HONOR THIS AFFIRMATION WHICH WILL PENETRATE TO THE VERY DEPTHS OF MY MIND, BODY, AND SPIRIT, IN THE SACRED NAME OF JESUS CHRIST, AMEN.

The following affirmations are a few of the tools that are extremely effective in countering the forces of evil. Of course, love is the basis for all the weapons God has designed to limit Satan's influence over us.

This next affirmation should be one of the first used:

"Heavenly Father, please forgive me for my sins, shortcomings, and imperfections, and reveal to me that they have been forgiven through faith and baptism. Help me to embrace and **activate my faith to forgive myself** which will help me perfect my life here on earth. I am now extremely determined to honor and obey this affirmation which will penetrate to the very depths of my mind, body, and spirit. In the sacred name of Jesus Christ, amen."

We should use only one or two affirmations at a session for righteous and unrighteous traits, attributes, and characteristics for a period of two weeks or more, repeating each of them consecutively four or five times with deep conviction for maximum effect.

Following is another format for righteously based affirmations:

"Heavenly Father, with the aid of Jesus Christ and the Holy Ghost, and with your unconditional love for me and me for them, please help me demonstrate **charity** for everyone when needed. Help me to always heed the promptings of the Holy Ghost and recognize when my aid is needed. Please help me to ever be aware of my need to be charitable in all situations where it is needed. This affirmation will now penetrate to the very depths of my mind, body, and spirit in the sacred name of Jesus Christ, amen."

CHAPTER FOURTEEN

Prayer Affirmations of Unifying Traits and Characteristics

WITH INTENSE FEELING AND CONVICTION, READ EACH SELECTED AFFIRMATION FOUR TIMES ALOUD ONCE A DAY FOR ONE MONTH, THEN SELECT ANOTHER:

1. ***DEITY*** – HEAVENLY FATHER, WITH THE AID OF JESUS CHRIST AND THE HOLY GHOST, AND WITH THEIR UNCONDITIONAL LOVE FOR ME AND ME FOR THEM, PLEASE HELP ME TO MAINTAIN THIS UNCONDITIONAL LOVE AND TO DEVELOP IT FOR ALL OF THY CHILDREN HERE ON EARTH. I WILL NOW ACCEPT AND APPLY THIS AFFIRMATION FROM THE VERY DEPTHS OF MY MIND, BODY, AND SPIRIT IN THE HOLY NAME OF JESUS CHRIST, AMEN.

2. ***ACTIVITY*** – HEAVENLY FATHER, WITH THE AID OF JESUS CHRIST AND THE HOLY GHOST, AND WITH THEIR UNCONDITIONAL LOVE FOR ME AND ME FOR THEM, PLEASE HELP ME RECOGNIZE THAT MY **ACTIVITY PROBLEM**

HAS BEEN A HARMFUL CHOICE BETWEEN THE HOLY GHOST AND SATAN'S FOLLOWERS. I WILL REASSESS MY PRIORITIES AND PLACE MY CONTINUED ACTIVITY HIGH ON THE LIST OF THINGS TO DO TO RETURN TO A GREAT RELATIONSHIP WITH THE HEAVENLY FATHER. WITH THY HELP, I NOW PLEDGE TO TAKE MY RESPONSIBILITY TO **BECOME AND STAY ACTIVE** IN MY CHURCH DUTIES VERY SERIOUSLY. FATHER, MAKE ME EVER AWARE OF RELYING ON THE HOLY GHOST TO KEEP ME ON THE RIGHT PATH TO THY KINGDOM. THIS AFFIRMATION WILL NOW PENETRATE TO THE VERY DEPTHS OF MY MIND, BODY, AND SPIRIT IN THE SACRED NAME OF JESUS CHRIST, AMEN.

3. *APPRECIATION* – HEAVENLY FATHER, WITH THE AID OF JESUS CHRIST AND THE HOLY GHOST, AND WITH THEIR UNCONDITIONAL LOVE FOR ME AND ME FOR THEM, PLEASE BLESS ME WITH THE FAITH, DESIRE, COURAGE, ABILITY, AND THE WILLINGNESS TO SHOW MY **APPRECIATION** FOR THE GOOD WORKS OF THOSE WITH WHOM I AM RESPONSIBLE. ALSO, PLEASE HELP ME TO CHOOSE THE PROMPTINGS OF THE HOLY GHOST INSTEAD OF SATAN. THIS ESSENTIAL AFFIRMATION WILL NOW PENETRATE TO THE VERY DEPTHS OF MY MIND, BODY, AND SPIRIT IN THE SACRED NAME OF JESUS CHRIST, AMEN.

4. *BENEVOLENCE* – HEAVENLY FATHER, WITH THE AID OF JESUS CHRIST AND THE HOLY GHOST, AND WITH THEIR UNCONDITIONAL LOVE FOR ME AND ME FOR THEM, PLEASE HELP ME TO RECOGNIZE THAT **BENEVOLENCE** HAS BEEN ONE OF MY FAILURES WHICH HAS LED ME TO

CHOOSE THE PROMPTINGS OF SATAN INSTEAD OF THE HOLY GHOST. PLEASE HELP ME TO MAKE THE CHANGES IN MY LIFE TO INCLUDE THE INCORPORATION OF **BENEVOLENCE** IN EVERY ASPECT OF MY LIFE. HELP ME TO EVER BE AWARE OF MY NEED TO RELY ON THE HOLY GHOST TO KEEP ME ON THE RIGHT PATH TO THY KINGDOM. THIS AFFIRMATION WILL NOW PENETRATE TO THE VERY DEPTHS OF MY MIND, BODY, AND SPIRIT IN THE SACRED NAME OF JESUS CHRIST, AMEN.

5. ***CHARITY*** – HEAVENLY FATHER, WITH THE AID OF JESUS CHRIST AND THE HOLY GHOST, AND WITH THEIR UNCONDITIONAL LOVE FOR ME AND ME FOR THEM, PLEASE HELP ME TO RECOGNIZE THAT **CHARITY** IS ONE OF THE MOST SOUGHT-AFTER TRAITS IN THIS WORLD AND THAT I NEED TO COMPLETELY INTEGRATE IT INTO MY PERSONALITY SO I CAN BETTER SERVE MY FAMILY, MY CHURCH, AND MY COMMUNITY. **CHARITY** IS THE PURE LOVE OF CHRIST, AND THOSE WHO ARE POSSESSED OF IT, ON THE JUDGMENT DAY, WILL RESIDE WITH GOD IN THE ETERNITIES. PLEASE HELP ME TO ALWAYS CHOOSE THE PROMPTINGS OF THE HOLY GHOST INSTEAD OF SATAN. THIS AFFIRMATION WILL NOW PENETRATE TO THE VERY DEPTHS OF MY MIND, BODY, AND SPIRIT IN THE SACRED NAME OF JESUS CHRIST, AMEN.

6. ***COMMITMENT*** – HEAVENLY FATHER, WITH THE AID OF JESUS CHRIST AND THE HOLY GHOST, AND WITH THEIR UNCONDITIONAL LOVE FOR ME AND ME FOR THEM, PLEASE HELP ME TO RECOGNIZE THAT **COMMITMENT** IS

ONE OF THE MOST DESIRABLE TRAITS IN THE INDUSTRIAL WORLD AND THAT I NEED TO COMPLETELY INTEGRATE IT INTO MY LIFE. PLEASE HELP ME TO ALWAYS CHOOSE THE PROMPTINGS OF THE HOLY GHOST, INSTEAD OF SATAN. HELP ME TO UNDERSTAND THAT **COMMITMENT** IN OBEYING GOD'S LAWS AND COMMANDMENTS IS ABSOLUTELY NECESSARY TO REGAIN THY KINGDOM AND RESIDE WITH THEE FOR ETERNITY. THIS AFFIRMATION WILL NOW PENETRATE TO THE VERY DEPTHS OF MY MIND, BODY, AND SPIRIT IN THE SACRED NAME OF JESUS CHRIST, AMEN.

7. *COMPASSION* – HEAVENLY FATHER, WITH THE AID OF JESUS CHRIST AND THE HOLY GHOST, AND WITH THEIR UNCONDITIONAL LOVE FOR ME AND ME FOR THEM, PLEASE HELP ME TO RECOGNIZE THAT **COMPASSION** IS ONE TRAIT THAT BRINGS AND HOLDS FAMILIES, ORGANIZATIONS, STATES, AND EVEN NATIONS TOGETHER. WITHOUT **COMPASSION**, THE FABRIC OF THESE GROUPS WOULD FALL APART JUST LIKE SATAN'S PLANS FOR ALL OF GOD'S CHILDREN. PLEASE HELP ME TO INTEGRATE THIS MUCH-DESIRED TRAIT INTO MY PERSONALITY AND MY LIFE. PLEASE HELP ME TO CHOOSE THE PROMPTINGS AND INFLUENCES OF THE HOLY GHOST INSTEAD OF SATAN. THIS AFFIRMATION WILL NOW PENETRATE TO THE VERY DEPTHS OF MY MIND, BODY, AND SPIRIT IN THE SACRED NAME OF JESUS CHRIST, AMEN.

8. *COURAGE* – HEAVENLY FATHER, WITH THE AID OF JESUS CHRIST AND THE HOLY GHOST, AND WITH THEIR UNCONDITIONAL LOVE

FOR ME AND ME FOR THEM, PLEASE HELP ME TO RECOGNIZE THE IMPORTANCE OF EXHIBITING **COURAGE** IN EVERY ASPECT OF MY LIFE, ESPECIALLY IN MAKING DECISIONS BASED ON THE PROMPTINGS OF THE HOLY GHOST INSTEAD OF SATAN. WITHOUT COURAGE, I WOULD BE AT THE MERCY OF SATAN EVERY MINUTE OF EVERY DAY. PLEASE BLESS ME WITH THE ACCEPTANCE AND RIGHTEOUS EXERCISE OF **COURAGE** IN EVERYTHING I DO. THIS AFFIRMATION WILL NOW PENETRATE TO THE VERY DEPTHS OF MY MIND, BODY, AND SPIRIT IN THE SACRED NAME OF JESUS CHRIST AMEN.

9. ***DEDICATION*** – HEAVENLY FATHER, WITH THE AID OF JESUS CHRIST AND THE HOLY GHOST, AND WITH THEIR UNCONDITIONAL LOVE FOR ME AND ME FOR THEM, PLEASE HELP ME TO BE MORE **DEDICATED** TO RIGHTEOUS ACTIVITIES. BLESS ME WITH THE FAITH, STRENGTH, DESIRE, COURAGE, ABILITY, AND THE WILLINGNESS TO OBEY THE PROMPTINGS OF THE HOLY GHOST INSTEAD OF THE FORCES OF EVIL AND HELP ME TO **DEDICATE** MY LIFE TO RIGHTEOUS ENDEAVORS. THIS AFFIRMATION WILL NOW PENETRATE TO THE VERY DEPTHS OF MY MIND, BODY, AND SPIRIT IN THE SACRED NAME OF JESUS CHRIST, AMEN.

10. ***FAITH*** – HEAVENLY FATHER, WITH THE AID OF JESUS CHRIST AND THE HOLY GHOST, AND WITH THEIR UNCONDITIONAL LOVE FOR ME AND ME FOR THEM, PLEASE BLESS ME WITH THE FAITH, DESIRE, COURAGE, ABILITY, AND THE WILLINGNESS TO RECOGNIZE THAT SATAN HAS BEEN INFLUENCING ME TO DIMINISH

MY USAGE OF **FAITH** IN EVERY ASPECT OF MY LIFE. PLEASE BLESS ME WITH THE STRENGTH AND DISCERNMENT NECESSARY TO FOLLOW THE PROMPTINGS OF THE HOLY GHOST IN PREFERENCE TO SATAN'S PROMPTINGS IN ALL OF MY ENDEAVORS. THIS AFFIRMATION WILL NOW PENETRATE TO THE VERY DEPTHS OF MY MIND, BODY, AND SPIRIT IN THE SACRED NAME OF JESUS CHRIST, AMEN.

11. ***FORGIVENESS*** – HEAVENLY FATHER, WITH THE AID OF JESUS CHRIST AND THE HOLY GHOST, AND WITH THEIR UNCONDITIONAL LOVE FOR ME AND ME FOR THEM, PLEASE BLESS ME WITH THE FAITH, DESIRE, COURAGE, ABILITY, AND THE WILLINGNESS TO BE **FORGIVING** IN ALL OF MY THOUGHTS AND ACTIONS. PLEASE HELP ME TO RECOGNIZE THAT SATAN IS THE INSTIGATOR OF OUR INABILITY TO **FORGIVE** PEOPLE OF THEIR OFFENSES AND RUMORED OFFENSES. PLEASE BLESS ME WITH THE DISCERNMENT NECESSARY TO COUNTER SATAN'S PROMPTINGS BY FOLLOWING THE INFLUENCES OF THE HOLY GHOST IN ALL ASPECTS OF MY LIFE. THIS ESSENTIAL AFFIRMATION WILL NOW PENETRATE TO THE VERY DEPTHS OF MY MIND, BODY, AND SPIRIT IN THE SACRED NAME OF JESUS CHRIST, AMEN.

12. ***GENTLENESS*** – HEAVENLY FATHER, WITH THE AID OF JESUS CHRIST AND THE HOLY GHOST, AND WITH THEIR UNCONDITIONAL LOVE FOR ME AND ME FOR THEM, PLEASE BLESS ME WITH THE FAITH, DESIRE, COURAGE, ABILITY, AND WILLINGNESS TO BE **GENTLE** TO EVERYONE WITH WHOM I COME IN CONTACT.

PLEASE HELP ME TO RECOGNIZE THAT SATAN HAS BEEN THE INFLUENCE PREVENTING ME FROM BEING **GENTLE AND CARING** AS I HAVE INTERACTED WITH MY FELLOW MAN. PLEASE BLESS ME WITH THE STRENGTH AND DISCERNMENT NECESSARY TO FOLLOW THE PROMPTINGS OF THE HOLY GHOST INSTEAD OF SATAN. THIS ESSENTIAL AFFIRMATION WILL NOW PENETRATE TO THE VERY DEPTHS OF MY MIND, BODY, AND SPIRIT IN THE SACRED NAME OF JESUS CHRIST, AMEN.

13. ***GODLINESS*** – HEAVENLY FATHER, WITH THE AID OF JESUS CHRIST AND THE HOLY GHOST, AND WITH THEIR UNCONDITIONAL LOVE FOR ME AND ME FOR THEM, PLEASE BLESS ME WITH THE FAITH, DESIRE, COURAGE, ABILITY, AND WILLINGNESS TO EMBRACE AND PERFECT THE TRAIT OF **GODLINESS** IN ALL ASPECTS OF MY LIFE. HELP ME TO FOLLOW THE PROMPTINGS OF THE HOLY GHOST INSTEAD OF SATAN'S. ALSO, HELP ME TO DISCERN THE DIFFERENCE. THIS ESSENTIAL AFFIRMATION WILL NOW PENETRATE TO THE VERY DEPTHS OF MY MIND, BODY, AND SPIRIT IN THE SACRED NAME OF JESUS CHRIST, AMEN.

14. ***HONESTY*** – HEAVENLY FATHER, WITH THE AID OF JESUS CHRIST AND THE HOLY GHOST, AND WITH THEIR UNCONDITIONAL LOVE FOR ME AND ME FOR THEM, PLEASE BLESS ME WITH THE FAITH, DESIRE, COURAGE, ABILITY, AND WILLINGNESS NECESSARY TO IDENTIFY AND COUNTER THE EFFECTS OF SATAN'S PROMPTINGS BY HEEDING THE INFLUENCES OF THE HOLY GHOST—TO BE **HONEST** IN

ALL OF MY RELATIONS WITH THOSE WHOM I INTERACT. THIS ESSENTIAL AFFIRMATION WILL NOW PENETRATE TO THE VERY DEPTHS OF MY MIND, BODY, AND SPIRIT IN THE SACRED NAME OF JESUS CHRIST, AMEN.

15. ***HONOR*** – HEAVENLY FATHER, WITH THE AID OF JESUS CHRIST AND THE HOLY GHOST, AND WITH THEIR UNCONDITIONAL LOVE FOR ME AND ME FOR THEM, PLEASE BLESS ME WITH THE FAITH, DESIRE, COURAGE, ABILITY, STRENGTH, AND WILLINGNESS TO MAGNIFY THE UNIFYING TRAIT OF **HONOR** IN MY LIFE AND HEED THE PROMPTINGS OF THE HOLY GHOST AND DIMINISH, EXPUNGE, AND ELIMINATE THE EFFECTS OF SATAN'S INFLUENCES TO DISCREDIT MY EFFORTS TO BE MORE HONORABLE. THIS AFFIRMATION WILL NOW PENETRATE TO THE VERY DEPTHS OF MY MIND, BODY, AND SPIRIT IN THE SACRED NAME OF JESUS CHRIST, AMEN.

16. ***HUMILITY*** – HEAVENLY FATHER, WITH THE AID OF JESUS CHRIST AND THE HOLY GHOST, AND WITH THEIR UNCONDITIONAL LOVE FOR ME AND ME FOR THEM, PLEASE BLESS ME WITH THE STRENGTH, FAITH, COURAGE, DESIRE, ABILITY, AND WILLINGNESS TO IDENTIFY AND ELIMINATE THE EFFECTS OF SATAN'S EFFORTS TO DIMINISH AND ERADICATE THE MUCH SOUGHT-AFTER TRAIT OF **HUMILITY**. HELP ME TO HEED THE PROMPTINGS OF THE HOLY GHOST INSTEAD OF SATAN'S PROMPTINGS IN MY EFFORTS TO PERFECT THIS IDEAL TRAIT. THIS ESSENTIAL AFFIRMATION WILL NOW PENETRATE TO THE VERY DEPTHS OF MY MIND,

BODY, AND SPIRIT IN THE SACRED NAME OF JESUS CHRIST, AMEN.

17. ***INTEGRITY*** – HEAVENLY FATHER, WITH THE AID OF JESUS CHRIST AND THE HOLY GHOST, AND WITH THEIR UNCONDITIONAL LOVE FOR ME AND ME FOR THEM, PLEASE BLESS ME WITH THE STRENGTH, FAITH, COURAGE, DESIRE, ABILITY, AND WILLINGNESS TO IDENTIFY AND ELIMINATE THE EFFECTS OF SATAN'S EFFORTS TO DIMINISH AND ERADICATE THE MUCH SOUGHT-AFTER TRAIT OF **INTEGRITY**. PLEASE HELP ME TO FOLLOW THE PROMPTINGS OF THE HOLY GHOST IN MY EFFORTS TO PERFECT THIS IDEAL TRAIT. THIS ESSENTIAL AFFIRMATION WILL NOW PENETRATE TO THE VERY DEPTHS OF MY MIND, BODY, AND SPIRIT IN THE SACRED NAME OF JESUS CHRIST, AMEN.

18. ***JUSTICE*** – HEAVENLY FATHER, WITH THE AID OF JESUS CHRIST AND THE HOLY GHOST, AND WITH THEIR UNCONDITIONAL LOVE FOR ME AND ME FOR THEM, PLEASE BLESS ME WITH THE STRENGTH, COURAGE, FAITH, ABILITY, DESIRE, AND WILLINGNESS TO IDENTIFY AND ELIMINATE THE EFFECTS OF SATAN'S EFFORTS TO DIMINISH AND ERADICATE MY DESIRE FOR **JUSTICE** IN MY EVERYDAY EXISTENCE. HELP ME TO ACT ON THE PROMPTINGS OF THE HOLY GHOST IN MY DETERMINATION TO RIGHTEOUSLY UTILIZE **JUSTICE** AS IT BECOMES NECESSARY IN MY LIFE. THIS ESSENTIAL AFFIRMATION WILL NOW PENETRATE TO THE VERY DEPTHS OF MY MIND, BODY, AND SPIRIT IN THE SACRED NAME OF JESUS CHRIST, AMEN.

19. **KINDNESS** – HEAVENLY FATHER, WITH THE AID OF JESUS CHRIST AND THE HOLY GHOST, AND WITH THEIR UNCONDITIONAL LOVE FOR ME AND ME FOR THEM, PLEASE BLESS ME WITH THE STRENGTH, COURAGE, DESIRE, FAITH, ABILITY, AND THE WILLINGNESS TO IDENTIFY AND ELIMINATE THE EFFECTS OF SATAN'S EFFORTS TO DIMINISH AND EXPUNGE MY NEED TO SHOW **KINDNESS** TO ALL THOSE WITH WHOM I COME IN CONTACT. PLEASE HELP ME TO ALWAYS ACT ON THE PROMPTINGS OF THE HOLY GHOST INSTEAD OF SATAN'S IN MY EFFORTS TO PERFECT MY EXPRESSION OF **KINDNESS** TOWARD EVERYONE. THIS ESSENTIAL AFFIRMATION WILL NOW PENETRATE TO THE VERY DEPTHS OF MY MIND, BODY, AND SPIRIT IN THE SACRED NAME OF JESUS CHRIST, AMEN.

20. **KNOWLEDGE** – HEAVENLY FATHER, WITH THE AID OF JESUS CHRIST AND THE HOLY GHOST, AND WITH THEIR UNCONDITIONAL LOVE FOR ME AND ME FOR THEM, PLEASE BLESS ME WITH THE STRENGTH, FAITH, COURAGE, DESIRE, ABILITY, AND WILLINGNESS TO IDENTIFY AND ELIMINATE THE EFFECTS OF SATAN'S EFFORTS THAT PREVENT ME FROM OBTAINING THE **KNOWLEDGE** I NEED TO REGAIN THY PRESENCE AND HEED THE PROMPTINGS OF THE HOLY GHOST, WHICH IS ABSOLUTELY NECESSARY TO OFFSET SATAN'S INFLUENCES. THIS ESSENTIAL AFFIRMATION WILL NOW PENETRATE TO THE VERY DEPTHS OF MY MIND, BODY, AND SPIRIT IN THE SACRED NAME OF JESUS CHRIST, AMEN.

21. **LOVE** – HEAVENLY FATHER, WITH THE AID OF JESUS CHRIST AND THE HOLY GHOST, AND

WITH THEIR UNCONDITIONAL LOVE FOR ME AND ME FOR THEM, PLEASE BLESS ME WITH THE STRENGTH, COURAGE, DESIRE, FAITH, AND WILLINGNESS TO IDENTIFY AND ELIMINATE THE EFFECTS OF SATAN'S EFFORTS IN PREVENTING ME FROM UNCONDITIONALLY **LOVING** GOD AND MY FELLOW MAN. I ABSOLUTELY NEED TO RECOGNIZE THE PROMPTINGS OF THE HOLY GHOST AND ABIDE BY HIS PROMPTINGS AND MASTER MY ABILITIES TO EXTEND **LOVE** TO EVERYONE. THIS ESSENTIAL AFFIRMATION WILL NOW PENETRATE TO THE VERY DEPTHS OF MY MIND, BODY, AND SPIRIT IN THE SACRED NAME OF JESUS CHRIST, AMEN.

22. ***MEEKNESS*** – HEAVENLY FATHER, WITH THE AID OF JESUS CHRIST AND HOLY GHOST, AND WITH THEIR UNCONDITIONAL LOVE FOR ME AND ME FOR THEM, PLEASE BLESS ME WITH THE STRENGTH, DESIRE, FAITH, COURAGE, ABILITY, AND WILLINGNESS TO IDENTIFY AND ELIMINATE THE EFFECTS OF SATAN'S EFFORTS TO PREVENT ME FROM BEING **MEEK** AND CARING FOR MY FELLOW MAN. I ABSOLUTELY NEED TO RECOGNIZE AND HEED THE PROMPTINGS OF THE HOLY GHOST WHICH HELPS ME TO MASTER MY ABILITY TO BE **MEEK** AND KIND TO EVERYONE I MEET. THIS ESSENTIAL AFFIRMATION WILL NOW PENETRATE TO THE VERY DEPTHS OF MY MIND, BODY, AND SPIRIT IN THE SACRED NAME OF JESUS CHRIST, AMEN.

23. ***MERCY*** – HEAVENLY FATHER, WITH THE AID OF JESUS CHRIST AND THE HOLY GHOST, AND WITH THEIR UNCONDITIONAL LOVE FOR ME AND ME FOR THEM, PLEASE BLESS ME WITH

THE ABILITY, STRENGTH, FAITH, COURAGE, DESIRE, AND WILLINGNESS TO EXTEND **MERCY** TO THOSE WHO HAVE OFFENDED ME IN ANY WAY AND TO RECOGNIZE THE INFLUENCE WHICH SATAN DEMONSTRATES IN LEADING ME AWAY FROM THE PROMPTINGS OF THE HOLY GHOST WHICH I MUST ALWAYS FOLLOW. THIS ESSENTIAL AFFIRMATION WILL NOW PENETRATE TO THE VERY DEPTHS OF MY MIND, BODY, AND SPIRIT IN THE SACRED NAME OF JESUS CHRIST, AMEN.

24. ***MODESTY*** – HEAVENLY FATHER, WITH THE AID OF JESUS CHRIST AND THE HOLY GHOST, AND WITH THEIR UNCONDITIONAL LOVE FOR ME AND ME FOR THEM, PLEASE BLESS ME WITH THE ABILITY, STRENGTH, FAITH, COURAGE, DESIRE, AND WILLINGNESS TO ALWAYS BE **MODEST** IN MY DRESS, ACTIONS, AND LANGUAGE WHEREVER AND WITH WHOMSOEVER I'M ASSOCIATED. PLEASE HELP ME TO ALWAYS BE AWARE THAT THE SATANIC FORCES ARE FOREVER TRYING TO PULL ME AWAY FROM THE PROMPTINGS OF THE HOLY GHOST AND MY DESIRE TO BE PERFECTED. THIS ESSENTIAL AFFIRMATION WILL NOW PENETRATE TO THE VERY DEPTHS OF MY MIND, BODY, AND SPIRIT IN THE SACRED NAME OF JESUS CHRIST, AMEN.

25. ***MORALITY*** – HEAVENLY FATHER, WITH THE AID OF JESUS CHRIST AND THE HOLY GHOST, AND WITH THEIR UNCONDITIONAL LOVE FOR ME AND ME FOR THEM, PLEASE BLESS ME WITH THE ABILITY, FAITH, STRENGTH, COURAGE, DESIRE, AND WILLINGNESS TO ALWAYS BE COMPLETELY **MORAL** IN ALL MY THINKING AND

ACTIVITIES. PLEASE HELP ME RECOGNIZE THE INFLUENCES SATAN BRINGS TO BEAR ON MY DESIRE TO PERFECT THIS WONDERFUL TRAIT. ALSO, PLEASE BLESS ME WITH THE ABILITY TO DISCERN THE DIFFERENCE BETWEEN THE PROMPTINGS OF SATANIC FORCES AND THE INFLUENCES OF THE HOLY GHOST AND BLESS ME WITH THE DESIRE TO ALWAYS SELECT AND HEED THE PROMPTINGS OF THE HOLY GHOST. THIS ESSENTIAL AFFIRMATION WILL NOW PENETRATE TO THE VERY DEPTHS OF MY MIND, BODY, AND SPIRIT IN THE SACRED NAME OF JESUS CHRIST, AMEN.

26. ***OBEDIENCE*** – HEAVENLY FATHER, WITH THE AID OF JESUS CHRIST AND THE HOLY GHOST, AND WITH THEIR UNCONDITIONAL LOVE FOR ME AND ME FOR THEM, PLEASE BLESS ME WITH THE COURAGE, FAITH, DETERMINATION, DESIRE STRENGTH, ABILITY, AND WILLINGNESS TO BE **OBEDIENT** TO ALL OF GOD'S LAWS AND COMMANDMENTS IN RESPONSE TO HEEDING THE PROMPTINGS OF THE HOLY GHOST AND IN PREFERENCE TO BEING **OBEDIENT** TO THE EVER-PRESENT SATANIC FORCES SURROUNDING ME. THIS ESSENTIAL AFFIRMATION WILL NOW PENETRATE TO THE VERY DEPTHS OF MY MIND, BODY, AND SPIRIT IN THE SACRED NAME OF JESUS CHRIST, AMEN.

27. ***REPENTANCE*** – HEAVENLY FATHER WITH THE AID OF JESUS CHRIST AND THE HOLY GHOST, AND WITH THEIR UNCONDITIONAL LOVE FOR ME AND ME FOR THEM, PLEASE BLESS ME WITH THE COURAGE, FAITH, ABILITY, DESIRE, AND WILLINGNESS TO CHOOSE THE FORCES OF THE

HOLY GHOST INSTEAD OF SATAN'S PROMPTINGS, WHICH WOULD DIMINISH MY DESIRE TO **REPENT**. PLEASE HELP ME TO **REPENT** AND REMAIN IN A STATE OF **REPENTANCE** FOR ALL OF MY SINS AND MISDEEDS. THIS AFFIRMATION WILL NOW PENETRATE TO THE VERY DEPTHS OF MY MIND, BODY, AND SPIRIT IN THE SACRED NAME OF JESUS CHRIST, AMEN.

28. *REVERENCE* – HEAVENLY FATHER, WITH THE AID OF JESUS CHRIST AND THE HOLY GHOST, AND WITH THEIR UNCONDITIONAL LOVE FOR ME AND ME FOR THEM, PLEASE BLESS ME WITH THE COURAGE, DESIRE, ABILITY, FAITH, AND THE WILLINGNESS TO BE **REVERENT** IN ALL OF MY THOUGHTS AND ACTIONS IN RESPONSE TO THE PROMPTINGS OF THE HOLY GHOST AND IN PREFERENCE OVER THOSE OF SATAN AND HIS MINIONS. THIS AFFIRMATION WILL NOW PENETRATE TO THE VERY DEPTHS OF MY MIND, BODY, AND SPIRIT IN THE SACRED NAME OF JESUS CHRIST, AMEN.

29. *RIGHTEOUSNESS* – HEAVENLY FATHER, WITH THE AID OF JESUS CHRIST AND THE HOLY GHOST, AND WITH THEIR UNCONDITIONAL LOVE FOR ME AND ME FOR THEM, PLEASE BLESS ME WITH THE FAITH, DESIRE, COURAGE, ABILITY, AND THE WILLINGNESS TO BE **RIGHTEOUS** IN ALL OF MY THOUGHTS AND ACTIONS IN RESPONSE TO THE PROMPTINGS OF THE HOLY GHOST AND IN PREFERENCE OVER THOSE OF SATAN AND HIS MINIONS. THIS AFFIRMATION WILL NOW PENETRATE TO THE VERY DEPTHS OF MY MIND, BODY, AND SPIRIT IN THE SACRED NAME OF JESUS CHRIST, AMEN.

30. ***SELF-ESTEEM*** – HEAVENLY FATHER, WITH THE AID OF JESUS CHRIST AND THE HOLY GHOST, AND WITH THEIR UNCONDITIONAL LOVE FOR ME AND ME FOR THEM, PLEASE BLESS ME WITH THE COURAGE, FAITH, ABILITY, DESIRE, AND THE WILLINGNESS TO DEMONSTRATE **SELF-ESTEEM** IN ALL OF MY THOUGHTS AND ACTIONS IN RESPONSE TO THE HOLY GHOST AND IN PREFERENCE OVER THE TEMPTATIONS AND PROMPTINGS OF SATAN AND HIS MINIONS. ALSO, PLEASE BLESS ME THAT I WON'T GIVE IN TO PRIDE AS SATAN WOULD HAVE ME DO. THIS AFFIRMATION WILL NOW PENETRATE TO THE VERY DEPTHS OF MY MIND, BODY, AND SPIRIT IN THE SACRED NAME OF JESUS CHRIST, AMEN.

31. ***SENSITIVITY*** – HEAVENLY FATHER, WITH THE AID OF JESUS CHRIST AND THE HOLY GHOST, AND WITH THEIR UNCONDITIONAL LOVE FOR ME AND ME FOR THEM, PLEASE BLESS ME WITH THE COURAGE, FAITH, DESIRE, ABILITY, AND WILLINGNESS TO BE **SENSITIVE** TO OTHER PEOPLE'S FEELINGS IN ALL OF MY THOUGHTS AND ACTIONS IN RESPONSE TO THE PROMPTINGS OF THE HOLY GHOST AND IN PREFERENCE OVER THE TEMPTATIONS AND INFLUENCES OF SATAN AND HIS MINIONS. THIS AFFIRMATION WILL NOW PENETRATE TO THE VERY DEPTHS OF MY MIND, BODY, AND SPIRIT, IN THE SACRED NAME OF JESUS CHRIST, AMEN.

32. ***SPIRITUALITY*** – HEAVENLY FATHER, WITH THE AID OF JESUS CHRIST AND THE HOLY GHOST, AND WITH THEIR UNCONDITIONAL LOVE FOR ME AND ME FOR THEM, PLEASE BLESS ME WITH THE COURAGE, FAITH, ABILITY, DESIRE, AND

THE WILLINGNESS TO ADAPT AND MAGNIFY MY **SPIRITUALITY** IN ALL OF MY THOUGHTS AND ACTIONS IN RESPONSE TO THE PROMPTINGS OF THE HOLY GHOST AND IN PREFERENCE TO THE TEMPTATIONS AND INFLUENCES OF SATAN AND HIS MINIONS. THIS AFFIRMATION WILL NOW PENETRATE TO THE VERY DEPTHS OF MY MIND, BODY, AND SPIRIT, IN THE SACRED NAME OF JESUS CHRIST, AMEN.

33. ***STABILITY*** – HEAVENLY FATHER, WITH THE AID OF JESUS CHRIST AND THE HOLY GHOST, AND WITH THEIR UNCONDITIONAL LOVE FOR ME AND ME FOR AND THEM, PLEASE BLESS ME WITH THE COURAGE, ABILITY, FAITH, DESIRE, AND THE WILLINGNESS TO BECOME **STABLE** IN ALL OF MY RIGHTEOUS THOUGHTS AND ACTIONS IN RESPONSE TO PROMPTINGS OF THE HOLY GHOST IN PREFERENCE TO THE INFLUENCES OF SATAN AND HIS MINIONS. THIS AFFIRMATION WILL NOW PENETRATE TO THE VERY DEPTHS OF MY MIND, BODY, AND SPIRIT, IN THE SACRED NAME OF JESUS CHRIST, AMEN.

34. ***TEMPERANCE*** – HEAVENLY FATHER, WITH THE AID OF JESUS CHRIST AND THE HOLY GHOST, AND WITH THEIR UNCONDITIONAL LOVE FOR ME AND ME FOR THEM, PLEASE BLESS ME WITH THE COURAGE, DESIRE, ABILITY, FAITH, AND THE WILLINGNESS TO BE **TEMPERATE** IN ALL OF MY THOUGHTS AND ACTIONS IN RESPONSE TO THE PROMPTINGS OF THE HOLY GHOST AND IN PREFERENCE TO THE TEMPTATIONS AND INFLUENCES OF SATAN AND HIS MINIONS. THIS AFFIRMATION WILL NOW PENETRATE TO THE

VERY DEPTHS OF MY MIND, BODY, AND SPIRIT, IN THE SACRED NAME OF JESUS CHRIST, AMEN.

35. **TRUST** – HEAVENLY FATHER, WITH THE AID OF JESUS CHRIST AND THE HOLY GHOST, AND WITH THEIR UNCONDITIONAL LOVE FOR ME AND ME FOR THEM, PLEASE BLESS ME WITH THE COURAGE, ABILITY, DESIRE, FAITH, AND THE WILLINGNESS TO ALWAYS PLACE MY COMPLETE **TRUST** IN GOD, JESUS CHRIST, AND THE HOLY GHOST REGARDLESS OF THEIR ACTIONS, BUT ONLY PLACE MY **TRUST** IN THE ARM OF A MAN WITH MUCH PRAYER AND SUPPLICATION AND WITH THE RESPONSE OF THE PROMPTINGS OF THE HOLY GHOST IN PREFERENCE TO THE TEMPTATIONS AND INFLUENCES OF SATAN AND HIS MINIONS. THIS AFFIRMATION WILL NOW PENETRATE TO THE VERY DEPTHS OF MY MIND, BODY, AND SPIRIT, IN THE SACRED NAME OF JESUS CHRIST, AMEN.

36. **VIRTUE** – HEAVENLY FATHER, WITH THE AID OF JESUS CHRIST AND THE HOLY GHOST, AND WITH THEIR UNCONDITIONAL LOVE FOR ME AND ME FOR THEM, PLEASE BLESS ME WITH THE COURAGE, DESIRE, ABILITY, FAITH, AND WILLINGNESS TO ALWAYS BE **VIRTUOUS** IN ALL OF MY THOUGHTS AND ACTIONS IN RESPONSE TO THE PROMPTINGS OF THE HOLY GHOST AND IN PREFERENCE TO THE TEMPTATIONS AND INFLUENCES OF SATAN AND HIS MINIONS. THIS AFFIRMATION WILL NOW PENETRATE TO THE VERY DEPTHS OF MY MIND, BODY, AND SPIRIT IN THE SACRED NAME OF JESUS CHRIST, AMEN.

The following affirmations are another format that has proved effective in helping to better perfect our lives:

37. HEAVENLY FATHER, WITH THE AID OF JESUS CHRIST AND THE HOLY GHOST, AND WITH THEIR UNCONDITIONAL LOVE FOR ME AND ME FOR THEM, PLEASE BLESS ME WITH THE COURAGE, ABILITY, FAITH, AND DESIRE TO EMBRACE AND ACTIVATE MY FAITH TO ADOPT, MAGNIFY, AND EXPAND THE FOLLOWING UNIFYING TRAITS AND CHARACTERISTICS—**CLEANLINESS**, **COMMITMENT**, AND **COMPASSION**—TO HELP PERFECT MY LIFE. I AM NOW EXTREMELY DETERMINED TO HONOR AND OBEY THIS AFFIRMATION, WHICH WILL NOW PENETRATE TO THE VERY DEPTHS OF MY MIND, BODY, AND SPIRIT IN THE SACRED NAME OF JESUS CHRIST, AMEN.

38. HEAVENLY FATHER, WITH THE AID OF JESUS CHRIST AND THE HOLY GHOST, AND WITH THEIR UNCONDITIONAL LOVE FOR ME AND ME FOR THEM, PLEASE BLESS ME WITH THE FAITH, COURAGE, ABILITY, AND DESIRE TO EMBRACE AND ACTIVATE MY FAITH TO ADOPT, MAGNIFY, AND EXPAND THE FOLLOWING UNIFYING TRAITS AND CHARACTERISTICS—**CONFIDENCE**, **CONSIDERATION**, AND **CONSISTENCY**—TO HELP PERFECT MY LIFE. I AM NOW EXTREMELY DETERMINED TO HONOR AND OBEY THIS AFFIRMATION, WHICH WILL PENETRATE TO THE VERY DEPTHS OF MY MIND, BODY, AND SPIRIT IN THE SACRED NAME OF JESUS CHRIST, AMEN.

39. HEAVENLY FATHER, WITH THE AID OF JESUS CHRIST AND THE HOLY GHOST, AND WITH UNCONDITIONAL LOVE FOR ME AND ME FOR THEM, PLEASE BLESS ME WITH THE ABILITY, COURAGE, FAITH, AND DESIRE TO EMBRACE AND ACTIVATE MY FAITH TO ADOPT, MAGNIFY, AND EXPAND THE FOLLOWING UNIFYING TRAITS AND CHARACTERISTICS—**COURAGE**, **CREATIVENESS**, AND **DEDICATION**—TO HELP PERFECT MY LIFE. I AM NOW EXTREMELY DETERMINED TO HONOR AND OBEY THIS AFFIRMATION, WHICH WILL PENETRATE TO THE VERY DEPTHS OF MY MIND, BODY, AND SPIRIT IN THE SACRED NAME OF JESUS CHRIST, AMEN.

40. HEAVENLY FATHER, WITH THE AID OF JESUS CHRIST AND THE HOLY GHOST, AND WITH THEIR UNCONDITIONAL LOVE FOR ME AND ME FOR THEM, PLEASE BLESS ME WITH THE ABILITY COURAGE, FAITH, AND DESIRE TO EMBRACE AND ACTIVATE MY FAITH TO ADOPT, MAGNIFY, AND EXPAND THE FOLLOWING UNIFYING TRAITS AND CHARACTERISTICS—**EQUALITY**, **FAITH**, AND **FORGIVENESS**—TO HELP PERFECT MY LIFE. I AM NOW EXTREMELY DETERMINED TO HONOR AND OBEY THIS AFFIRMATION, WHICH WILL PENETRATE TO THE VERY DEPTHS OF MY MIND, BODY, AND SPIRIT IN THE SACRED NAME OF JESUS CHRIST, AMEN.

41. HEAVENLY FATHER, WITH THE AID OF JESUS CHRIST AND THE HOLY GHOST, AND WITH THEIR UNCONDITIONAL LOVE FOR ME AND ME FOR THEM, PLEASE BLESS ME WITH THE ABILITY, COURAGE, FAITH, AND DESIRE TO

EMBRACE AND ACTIVATE MY FAITH TO ADOPT, MAGNIFY, AND EXPAND THE FOLLOWING UNIFYING TRAITS AND CHARACTERISTICS—**FRIENDLINESS**, **GOAL-SEEKING TRAIT**, AND **GENTLENESS**—TO HELP PERFECT MY LIFE. I AM NOW EXTREMELY DETERMINED TO HONOR AND OBEY THIS AFFIRMATION, WHICH WILL PENETRATE TO THE VERY DEPTHS OF MY MIND, BODY, AND SPIRIT IN THE SACRED NAME OF JESUS CHRIST, AMEN.

42. HEAVENLY FATHER, WITH THE AID OF JESUS CHRIST AND THE HOLY GHOST, AND WITH THEIR UNCONDITIONAL LOVE FOR ME AND ME FOR THEM, PLEASE BLESS ME WITH THE ABILITY, COURAGE, FAITH, AND DESIRE TO EMBRACE AND ACTIVATE MY FAITH TO ADOPT, MAGNIFY, AND EXPAND THE FOLLOWING UNIFYING TRAITS AND CHARACTERISTICS—**GODLINESS**, **HELPFULNESS**, AND **HONESTY**—TO HELP PERFECT MY LIFE. I AM NOW EXTREMELY DETERMINED TO HONOR AND OBEY THIS AFFIRMATION, WHICH WILL PENETRATE TO THE VERY DEPTHS OF MY MIND, BODY, AND SPIRIT, IN THE SACRED NAME OF JESUS CHRIST, AMEN.

43. HEAVENLY FATHER, WITH THE AID OF JESUS CHRIST AND THE HOLY GHOST, AND WITH THEIR UNCONDITIONAL LOVE FOR ME AND ME FOR THEM, PLEASE BLESS ME WITH THE ABILITY, COURAGE, FAITH, AND DESIRE TO EMBRACE AND ACTIVATE MY FAITH TO ADOPT, MAGNIFY, AND EXPAND THE FOLLOWING UNIFYING TRAITS AND CHARACTERISTICS—**HONOR**, **HOPE**, AND **HUMILITY**—TO HELP PERFECT MY

LIFE. I AM NOW EXTREMELY DETERMINED TO HONOR AND OBEY THIS AFFIRMATION, WHICH WILL PENETRATE TO THE VERY DEPTHS OF MY MIND, BODY, AND SPIRIT IN THE SACRED NAME OF JESUS CHRIST, AMEN.

44. HEAVENLY FATHER, WITH THE AID OF JESUS CHRIST AND THE HOLY GHOST, AND WITH THEIR UNCONDITIONAL LOVE FOR ME AND ME FOR THEM, PLEASE BLESS ME WITH THE ABILITY, COURAGE, FAITH, AND DESIRE TO EMBRACE AND ACTIVATE MY FAITH TO ADOPT, MAGNIFY, AND EXPAND THE FOLLOWING UNIFYING TRAITS AND CHARACTERISTICS—**HUMOR**, **INDUSTRY**, AND **INQUISITIVENESS**—TO HELP PERFECT MY LIFE. I AM NOW EXTREMELY DETERMINED TO HONOR AND OBEY THIS AFFIRMATION, WHICH WILL PENETRATE TO THE VERY DEPTHS OF MY MIND, BODY, AND SPIRIT IN THE SACRED NAME OF JESUS CHRIST, AMEN.

45. HEAVENLY FATHER, WITH THE AID OF JESUS CHRIST AND THE HOLY GHOST, AND WITH THEIR UNCONDITIONAL LOVE FOR ME AND ME FOR THEM, PLEASE BLESS ME WITH THE ABILITY, COURAGE, FAITH, AND DESIRE TO EMBRACE AND ACTIVATE MY FAITH TO ADOPT, MAGNIFY, AND EXPAND THE FOLLOWING UNIFYING TRAITS AND CHARACTERISTICS—**INTEGRITY**, **INTENTION**, AND **JUSTICE**—TO HELP PERFECT MY LIFE. I AM NOW EXTREMELY DETERMINED TO HONOR AND OBEY THIS AFFIRMATION, WHICH WILL PENETRATE TO THE VERY DEPTHS OF MY MIND, BODY, AND SPIRIT IN THE SACRED NAME OF JESUS CHRIST, AMEN.

46. HEAVENLY FATHER, WITH THE AID OF JESUS CHRIST AND THE HOLY GHOST, AND WITH THEIR UNCONDITIONAL LOVE FOR ME AND ME FOR THEM, PLEASE BLESS ME WITH THE ABILITY, COURAGE, FAITH, AND DESIRE TO EMBRACE AND ACTIVATE MY FAITH TO ADOPT, MAGNIFY, AND EXPAND THE FOLLOWING UNIFYING TRAITS AND CHARACTERISTICS—**KINDNESS**, **KNOWLEDGE**, AND **LOVE**—TO HELP PERFECT MY LIFE. I AM NOW EXTREMELY DETERMINED TO HONOR AND OBEY THIS AFFIRMATION, WHICH WILL PENETRATE TO THE VERY DEPTHS OF MY MIND, BODY, AND SPIRIT IN THE SACRED NAME OF JESUS CHRIST, AMEN.

47. HEAVENLY FATHER, WITH THE AID OF JESUS CHRIST AND THE HOLY GHOST, AND WITH THEIR UNCONDITIONAL LOVE FOR ME AND ME FOR THEM, PLEASE BLESS ME WITH THE ABILITY, COURAGE, FAITH, AND DESIRE TO EMBRACE AND ACTIVATE MY FAITH, TO ADOPT, MAGNIFY, AND EXPAND THE FOLLOWING UNIFYING TRAITS AND CHARACTERISTICS—**LOYALTY**, **MEEKNESS**, AND **MERCY**—TO HELP PERFECT MY LIFE. I AM NOW EXTREMELY DETERMINED TO HONOR AND OBEY THIS AFFIRMATION, WHICH WILL NOW PENETRATE TO THE VERY DEPTHS OF MY MIND, BODY, AND SPIRIT IN THE SACRED NAME OF JESUS CHRIST, AMEN.

48. HEAVENLY FATHER, WITH THE AID OF JESUS CHRIST AND THE HOLY GHOST, AND WITH THEIR UNCONDITIONAL LOVE FOR ME AND ME FOR THEM, PLEASE BLESS ME WITH THE ABILITY, COURAGE, FAITH, AND DESIRE TO EMBRACE AND ACTIVATE MY FAITH, TO ADOPT,

MAGNIFY, AND EXPAND THE FOLLOWING UNIFYING TRAITS AND CHARACTERISTICS—**MEDITATION**, **MODESTY**, AND **MORALITY**—TO HELP PERFECT MY LIFE. I AM NOW EXTREMELY DETERMINED TO HONOR AND OBEY THIS AFFIRMATION, WHICH WILL NOW PENETRATE TO THE VERY DEPTHS OF MY MIND, BODY, AND SPIRIT IN THE SACRED NAME OF JESUS CHRIST, AMEN.

49. HEAVENLY FATHER, WITH THE AID OF JESUS CHRIST AND THE HOLY GHOST, AND WITH THEIR UNCONDITIONAL LOVE FOR ME AND ME FOR THEM, PLEASE BLESS ME WITH THE ABILITY, COURAGE, FAITH, AND DESIRE TO EMBRACE AND EXERCISE MY FAITH, TO ADOPT, MAGNIFY, AND EXPAND THE FOLLOWING UNIFYING TRAITS AND CHARACTERISTICS—**MOTIVATION**, **OBEDIENCE**, AND **ORGANIZATION**—TO HELP PERFECT MY LIFE. I AM NOW EXTREMELY DETERMINED TO HONOR AND OBEY THIS AFFIRMATION, WHICH WILL PENETRATE TO THE VERY DEPTHS OF MY MIND, BODY, AND SPIRIT, IN THE SACRED NAME OF JESUS CHRIST, AMEN.

50. HEAVENLY FATHER, WITH THE AID OF JESUS CHRIST AND THE HOLY GHOST, AND WITH THEIR UNCONDITIONAL LOVE FOR ME AND ME FOR THEM, PLEASE BLESS ME WITH THE ABILITY, COURAGE, FAITH, AND DESIRE TO EMBRACE AND EXERCISE MY FAITH, TO ADOPT, MAGNIFY, AND EXPAND THE FOLLOWING UNIFYING TRAITS AND CHARACTERISTICS—**PATIENCE**, **PERSISTENCE**, AND **PREPAREDNESS** TO HELP PERFECT MY LIFE. I AM NOW EXTREMELY

DETERMINED TO HONOR AND OBEY THIS AFFIRMATION, WHICH WILL PENETRATE TO THE VERY DEPTHS OF MY MIND, BODY, AND SPIRIT, IN THE SACRED NAME OF JESUS CHRIST, AMEN.

51. HEAVENLY FATHER, WITH THE AID OF JESUS CHRIST AND THE HOLY GHOST, AND WITH THEIR UNCONDITIONAL LOVE FOR ME AND ME FOR THEM, PLEASE BLESS ME WITH THE ABILITY, COURAGE, FAITH, AND DESIRE TO EMBRACE AND EXERCISE MY FAITH, TO ADOPT, MAGNIFY, AND EXPAND THE FOLLOWING UNIFYING TRAITS AND CHARACTERISTICS—**PROMPTNESS**, **PURITY**, AND **REPENTANCE**—TO HELP PERFECT MY LIFE. I AM NOW EXTREMELY DETERMINED TO HONOR AND OBEY THIS AFFIRMATION, WHICH WILL PENETRATE TO THE VERY DEPTHS OF MY MIND, BODY, AND SPIRIT IN THE SACRED NAME OF JESUS CHRIST, AMEN.

52. HEAVENLY FATHER, WITH THE AID OF JESUS CHRIST AND THE HOLY GHOST, AND WITH THEIR UNCONDITIONAL LOVE FOR ME AND ME FOR THEM, PLEASE BLESS ME WITH THE ABILITY, COURAGE, FAITH, AND DESIRE TO EMBRACE AND EXERCISE MY FAITH TO ADOPT, MAGNIFY, AND EXPAND THE FOLLOWING UNIFYING TRAITS AND CHARACTERISTICS—**RESILIENCE**, **RESOLUTION**, AND **RESPONSIBILITY** TO HELP PERFECT MY LIFE. I AM NOW EXTREMELY DETERMINED TO HONOR AND OBEY THIS AFFIRMATION, WHICH WILL PENETRATE TO THE VERY DEPTHS OF MY MIND, BODY, AND SPIRIT, IN THE SACRED NAME OF JESUS CHRIST, AMEN.

53. HEAVENLY FATHER, WITH THE AID OF JESUS CHRIST AND THE HOLY GHOST, AND WITH THEIR UNCONDITIONAL LOVE FOR ME AND ME FOR THEM, PLEASE BLESS ME WITH THE ABILITY, COURAGE, FAITH, AND DESIRE TO EMBRACE AND EXERCISE MY FAITH TO ADOPT, MAGNIFY, AND EXPAND THE FOLLOWING UNIFYING TRAITS AND CHARACTERISTICS—**REVERENCE**, **RIGHTEOUSNESS**, AND **SACRIFICE**—TO HELP PERFECT MY LIFE. I AM NOW EXTREMELY DETERMINED TO HONOR AND OBEY THIS AFFIRMATION, WHICH WILL PENETRATE TO THE VERY DEPTHS OF MY MIND, BODY, AND SPIRIT IN THE SACRED NAME OF JESUS CHRIST, AMEN.

54. HEAVENLY FATHER, WITH THE AID OF JESUS CHRIST AND THE HOLY GHOST, AND WITH THEIR UNCONDITIONAL LOVE FOR ME AND ME FOR THEM, PLEASE BLESS ME WITH THE ABILITY, COURAGE, FAITH, AND DESIRE TO EMBRACE AND ACTIVATE MY FAITH, TO ACCEPT, MAGNIFY, AND EXPAND THE FOLLOWING UNIFYING TRAITS AND CHARACTERISTICS—**DISCIPLINE**, **SELF-ESTEEM**, AND **SELF-RELIANCE**—TO HELP PERFECT MY LIFE. I AM NOW EXTREMELY DETERMINED TO HONOR AND OBEY THIS AFFIRMATION, WHICH WILL PENETRATE TO THE VERY DEPTHS OF MY MIND, BODY, AND SPIRIT IN THE SACRED NAME OF JESUS CHRIST, AMEN.

55. HEAVENLY FATHER, WITH THE AID OF JESUS CHRIST AND THE HOLY GHOST, AND WITH THEIR UNCONDITIONAL LOVE FOR ME AND ME FOR THEM, PLEASE BLESS ME WITH THE ABILITY,

COURAGE, FAITH, AND DESIRE TO EMBRACE AND ACTIVATE MY FAITH, TO ADOPT, MAGNIFY, AND EXPAND THE FOLLOWING UNIFYING TRAITS AND CHARACTERISTICS—**SENSITIVITY, SERENITY,** AND **SHARING**—TO HELP PERFECT MY LIFE. I AM NOW EXTREMELY DETERMINED TO HONOR AND OBEY THIS AFFIRMATION, WHICH WILL PENETRATE TO THE VERY DEPTHS OF MY MIND, BODY, AND SPIRIT IN THE SACRED NAME OF JESUS CHRIST, AMEN.

56. HEAVENLY FATHER, WITH THE AID OF JESUS CHRIST AND THE HOLY GHOST, AND WITH THEIR UNCONDITIONAL LOVE FOR ME AND ME FOR THEM, PLEASE BLESS ME WITH THE ABILITY, COURAGE, FAITH, AND DESIRE TO EMBRACE AND ACTIVATE MY FAITH TO ADOPT, MAGNIFY, AND EXPAND THE FOLLOWING UNIFYING TRAITS AND CHARACTERISTICS—**SPIRITUALITY, STABILITY,** AND **STEADFASTNESS**—TO HELP PERFECT MY LIFE. I AM NOW EXTREMELY DETERMINED TO HONOR AND OBEY THIS AFFIRMATION, WHICH WILL PENETRATE TO THE VERY DEPTHS OF MY MIND, BODY, AND SPIRIT IN THE SACRED NAME OF JESUS CHRIST, AMEN.

57. HEAVENLY FATHER, WITH THE AID OF JESUS CHRIST AND THE HOLY GHOST, AND WITH THEIR UNCONDITIONAL LOVE FOR ME AND ME FOR THEM, PLEASE HELP ME WITH THE ABILITY, COURAGE, FAITH, AND DESIRE TO EMBRACE AND ACTIVATE MY FAITH TO ADOPT, MAGNIFY, AND EXPAND THE FOLLOWING UNIFYING TRAITS AND CHARACTERISTICS—**STRENGTH, STUDIOUSNESS,** AND **SUCCESS**

ORIENTATION—TO HELP PERFECT MY LIFE. I AM NOW EXTREMELY DETERMINED TO HONOR AND OBEY THIS AFFIRMATION, WHICH WILL PENETRATE TO THE VERY DEPTHS OF MY MIND, BODY, AND SPIRIT IN THE SACRED NAME OF JESUS CHRIST, AMEN.

58. HEAVENLY FATHER, WITH THE AID OF JESUS CHRIST AND THE HOLY GHOST, AND WITH THEIR UNCONDITIONAL LOVE FOR ME AND ME FOR THEM, PLEASE BLESS ME WITH THE ABILITY AND DESIRE TO EMBRACE AND ACTIVATE MY FAITH TO ADOPT, MAGNIFY, AND EXPAND THE FOLLOWING UNIFYING TRAITS AND CHARACTERISTICS—**TACT**, **SURRENDERING**, AND **TEMPERANCE**—TO HELP PERFECT MY LIFE. I AM NOW EXTREMELY DETERMINED TO HONOR AND OBEY THIS AFFIRMATION, WHICH WILL PENETRATE TO THE VERY DEPTHS OF MY MIND, BODY, AND SPIRIT IN THE SACRED NAME OF JESUS CHRIST, AMEN.

59. HEAVENLY FATHER, WITH THE AID OF JESUS CHRIST AND THE HOLY GHOST, AND WITH THEIR UNCONDITIONAL LOVE FOR ME AND ME FOR THEM, PLEASE BLESS ME WITH THE ABILITY AND DESIRE TO EMBRACE AND ACTIVATE MY FAITH TO ADOPT, MAGNIFY, AND EXPAND THE FOLLOWING UNIFYING TRAITS AND CHARACTERISTICS—**TRUST**, **THOUGHTFULNESS**, **VIRTUE**, AND **WATCHFULNESS**—TO HELP PERFECT MY LIFE. I AM NOW EXTREMELY DETERMINED TO HONOR AND OBEY THIS AFFIRMATION, WHICH WILL PENETRATE TO THE VERY DEPTHS OF MY MIND, BODY, AND SPIRIT IN THE SACRED NAME OF JESUS CHRIST, AMEN.

60. **ANGER** – HEAVENLY FATHER, WITH THE AID OF JESUS CHRIST AND THE HOLY GHOST, AND WITH THEIR UNCONDITIONAL LOVE FOR ME AND ME FOR THEM, PLEASE BLESS ME WITH THE DESIRE, ABILITY, FAITH, COURAGE, AND THE WILLINGNESS TO REALIZE THAT **ANGER** IS THE RESULT OF HEEDING THE PROMPTINGS OF SATAN AND HIS MINIONS AND THAT I NEED TO RELY ON THE PROMPTINGS OF THE HOLY GHOST TO CONTROL AND EXPUNGE IT FROM MY EVERYDAY USAGE. THIS AFFIRMATION WILL NOW PENETRATE TO THE VERY DEPTHS OF MY MIND, BODY, AND SPIRIT IN THE SACRED NAME OF JESUS CHRIST, AMEN.

61. **CHEATING** – HEAVENLY FATHER, WITH THE AID OF JESUS CHRIST AND THE HOLY GHOST, AND WITH THEIR UNCONDITIONAL LOVE FOR ME AND ME FOR THEM, PLEASE BLESS ME WITH THE DESIRE, FAITH, COURAGE, ABILITY, AND THE WILLINGNESS TO ELIMINATE AND EXPUNGE THE EVIL TRAIT OF **CHEATING** FROM MY DAY TO DAY USAGE, WHICH IS THE RESULT OF HEEDING THE PROMPTINGS OF THE DEVIL AND HIS MINIONS IN PREFERENCE TO THOSE OF THE HOLY GHOST. THIS AFFIRMATION WILL NOW PENETRATE TO THE VERY DEPTHS OF MY MIND, BODY, AND SPIRIT IN THE SACRED NAME OF JESUS CHRIST, AMEN.

62. **CONTENTION** – HEAVENLY FATHER, WITH THE AID OF JESUS CHRIST AND THE HOLY GHOST, AND WITH THEIR UNCONDITIONAL LOVE FOR ME AND ME FOR THEM, PLEASE BLESS ME WITH THE DESIRE, FAITH, COURAGE, ABILITY, AND THE WILLINGNESS TO REALIZE THAT

CONTENTION IS ONE OF THE MOST USED EVIL TRAITS OF SATAN AND HIS MINIONS, AND THAT I NEED TO RELY ON THE PROMPTINGS OF THE HOLY GHOST TO CONTROL AND EXPUNGE IT FROM MY PERSONALITY IN PREFERENCE TO THE INFLUENCES OF THE DEVIL AND HIS HOARDS. THIS AFFIRMATION WILL NOW PENETRATE TO THE VERY DEPTHS OF MY MIND, BODY, AND SPIRIT IN THE SACRED NAME OF JESUS CHRIST, AMEN.

63. ***COWARDICE*** – HEAVENLY FATHER, WITH THE AID OF JESUS CHRIST AND THE HOLY GHOST, AND WITH THEIR UNCONDITIONAL LOVE FOR ME AND ME FOR THEM, PLEASE BLESS ME WITH THE DESIRE, FAITH, COURAGE, ABILITY, AND WILLINGNESS TO REALIZE THAT **COWARDICE** IS CENTERED IN FEAR AND IS ANOTHER EVIL TRAIT SATAN AND HIS MINIONS CULTIVATE IN HIS HUMAN PUPPETS, AND THAT I NEED TO RELY ON THE PROMPTINGS OF THE HOLY GHOST TO CONTROL AND EXPUNGE IT FROM MY PERSONA IN PREFERENCE TO THE INFLUENCES OF THE DEVIL AND HIS HOARDS. THIS AFFIRMATION WILL NOW PENETRATE TO THE VERY DEPTHS OF MY MIND, BODY, AND SPIRIT IN THE SACRED NAME OF JESUS CHRIST, AMEN.

64. ***CRUELTY*** – HEAVENLY FATHER, WITH THE AID OF JESUS CHRIST AND THE HOLY GHOST, AND WITH THEIR UNCONDITIONAL LOVE FOR ME AND ME FOR THEM, PLEASE BLESS ME WITH THE DESIRE, FAITH, COURAGE, ABILITY, AND THE WILLINGNESS TO REALIZE THAT **CRUELTY** IS ANOTHER OF SATAN'S MOST EVIL AND MOST USED TRAIT TO PUNISH US, HUMANS, FOR NOT

FOLLOWING HIM IN THE SPIRIT WORLD. PLEASE BLESS ME WITH THE DESIRE, ABILITY, COURAGE, FAITH, AND WILLINGNESS TO FOLLOW THE PROMPTINGS OF THE HOLY GHOST INSTEAD OF THE DEVIL'S INFLUENCE. THIS AFFIRMATION WILL NOW PENETRATE TO THE VERY DEPTHS OF MY MIND, BODY, AND SPIRIT IN THE SACRED NAME OF JESUS CHRIST, AMEN.

65. **DISHONESTY** – HEAVENLY FATHER, WITH THE AID OF JESUS CHRIST AND THE HOLY GHOST, AND WITH THEIR UNCONDITIONAL LOVE FOR ME AND ME FOR THEM, PLEASE BLESS ME WITH THE DESIRE, FAITH, COURAGE, ABILITY, AND THE WILLINGNESS TO LISTEN TO AND HEED THE PROMPTINGS OF THE HOLY GHOST IN PREFERENCE TO THOSE OF THE DEVIL, AND ALWAYS DEFEAT SATAN IN HIS EFFORTS TO INDUCE ME TO BE **DISHONEST**. THIS AFFIRMATION WILL PENETRATE TO THE VERY DEPTHS OF MY MIND, BODY, AND SPIRIT IN THE SACRED NAME OF JESUS CHRIST, AMEN.

66. **DISLOYALTY** – HEAVENLY FATHER, WITH THE AID OF JESUS CHRIST AND THE HOLY GHOST, AND WITH THEIR UNCONDITIONAL LOVE FOR ME AND ME FOR THEM, PLEASE BLESS ME WITH THE ABILITY, DESIRE, FAITH, COURAGE, AND WILLINGNESS TO LISTEN TO AND HEED THE PROMPTINGS OF THE HOLY GHOST IN PREFERENCE TO THOSE OF THE DEVIL AND ALWAYS DEFEAT HIM IN HIS EFFORTS TO INDUCE ME TO BE **DISLOYAL**. THIS AFFIRMATION WILL NOW PENETRATE TO THE VERY DEPTHS OF MY MIND, BODY, AND SPIRIT IN THE SACRED NAME OF JESUS CHRIST, AMEN.

67. ***DISOBEDIENCE*** – HEAVENLY FATHER, WITH THE AID OF JESUS CHRIST AND THE HOLY GHOST, AND WITH THEIR UNCONDITIONAL LOVE FOR ME AND ME FOR THEM, PLEASE BLESS ME WITH THE ABILITY, DESIRE, FAITH, COURAGE, AND THE WILLINGNESS TO LISTEN TO AND HEED THE PROMPTINGS OF THE HOLY GHOST IN PREFERENCE TO THOSE OF THE DEVIL, AND ALWAYS DEFEAT HIM IN HIS EFFORTS TO INDUCE ME TO BE **DISOBEDIENT** TO GOD'S LAWS AND COMMANDMENT. THIS AFFIRMATION WILL NOW PENETRATE TO THE VERY DEPTHS OF MY MIND, BODY, AND SPIRIT IN THE SACRED NAME OF JESUS CHRIST, AMEN.

68. ***DESTRUCTION*** – HEAVENLY FATHER, WITH THE AID OF JESUS CHRIST AND THE HOLY GHOST, AND WITH THEIR UNCONDITIONAL LOVE FOR ME AND ME FOR THEM, PLEASE BLESS ME WITH THE ABILITY, DESIRE, FAITH, COURAGE, AND WILLINGNESS TO LISTEN TO AND HEED THE PROMPTINGS OF THE HOLY GHOST IN PREFERENCE TO THOSE OF THE DEVIL AND ALWAYS DEFEAT HIM IN HIS EFFORTS TO INDUCE ME TO BE **DESTRUCTIVE** TO THOSE WITH WHOM I LOVE AND COME IN CONTACT. THIS AFFIRMATION WILL NOW PENETRATE TO THE VERY DEPTHS OF MY MIND, BODY, AND SPIRIT IN THE SACRED NAME OF JESUS CHRIST, AMEN.

69. ***DOUBT*** – HEAVENLY FATHER, WITH THE AID OF JESUS CHRIST AND THE HOLY GHOST, AND WITH THEIR UNCONDITIONAL LOVE FOR ME AND ME FOR THEM, PLEASE BLESS ME WITH THE ABILITY, DESIRE, FAITH, COURAGE, AND

WILLINGNESS TO HEED THE PROMPTINGS OF THE HOLY GHOST IN PREFERENCE TO THOSE OF THE DEVIL AND HIS MINIONS AND ALWAYS DEFEAT HIM IN HIS EFFORTS TO CREATE **DOUBT** IN MY RIGHTEOUS THOUGHTS, ENDEAVORS, AND ACTIVITIES. THIS AFFIRMATION WILL NOW PENETRATE TO THE VERY DEPTHS OF MY MIND, BODY, AND SPIRIT IN THE SACRED NAME OF JESUS CHRIST, AMEN.

70. ***ENMITY*** – HEAVENLY FATHER, WITH THE AID OF JESUS CHRIST AND THE HOLY GHOST, AND WITH THEIR UNCONDITIONAL LOVE FOR ME AND ME FOR THEM, PLEASE BLESS ME WITH THE ABILITY, DESIRE, FAITH, COURAGE, AND THE WILLINGNESS TO HEED THE PROMPTINGS OF THE HOLY GHOST IN PREFERENCE TO THOSE OF THE DEVIL AND HIS MINIONS AND ALWAYS DEFEAT HIM IN HIS EFFORTS TO CREATE **ENMITY** BETWEEN ME AND MY ASSOCIATION WITH OTHERS. THIS AFFIRMATION WILL NOW PENETRATE TO THE VERY DEPTHS OF MY MIND, BODY, AND SPIRIT IN THE SACRED NAME OF JESUS CHRIST, AMEN.

71. ***ENVYING*** – HEAVENLY FATHER, WITH THE AID OF JESUS CHRIST AND THE HOLY GHOST, AND WITH THEIR UNCONDITIONAL LOVE FOR ME AND ME FOR THEM, PLEASE BLESS ME WITH THE ABILITY, DESIRE, FAITH, COURAGE, AND WILLINGNESS TO LISTEN TO AND HEED THE PROMPTINGS OF THE HOLY GHOST IN PREFERENCE TO THOSE OF THE DEVIL AND HIS MINIONS AND ALWAYS DEFEAT HIM IN HIS EFFORTS TO INDUCE ME TO **ENVY** OTHERS IN WHAT THEY HAVE OR WHAT THEY ARE. THIS

AFFIRMATION WILL NOW PENETRATE TO THE VERY DEPTHS OF MY MIND, BODY, AND SPIRIT IN THE SACRED NAME OF JESUS CHRIST, AMEN.

72. **GOSSIP** – HEAVENLY FATHER, WITH THE AID OF JESUS CHRIST AND THE HOLY GHOST, AND WITH THEIR UNCONDITIONAL LOVE FOR ME AND ME FOR THEM, PLEASE BLESS ME WITH THE FAITH, COURAGE, ABILITY, DESIRE, AND WILLINGNESS TO LISTEN TO AND HEED THE PROMPTINGS OF THE HOLY GHOST IN PREFERENCE TO THE DEVIL AND HIS MINIONS AND DEFEAT HIM IN HIS EFFORTS TO ENTICE ME TO **GOSSIP** ABOUT OTHERS AND DESTROY THEIR REPUTATIONS OR MAKE MYSELF LOOK BETTER THAN THEM. THIS AFFIRMATION WILL NOW PENETRATE TO THE VERY DEPTHS OF MY MIND, BODY, AND SPIRIT IN THE SACRED NAME OF JESUS CHRIST, AMEN.

73. **GREED** – HEAVENLY FATHER, WITH THE AID OF JESUS CHRIST AND THE HOLY GHOST, AND WITH THEIR UNCONDITIONAL LOVE FOR ME AND ME FOR THEM, PLEASE BLESS ME WITH THE FAITH, COURAGE, ABILITY, DESIRE, AND THE WILLINGNESS TO LISTEN TO AND HEED THE PROMPTINGS OF THE HOLY GHOST IN PREFERENCE TO THE DEVIL AND HIS MINIONS, AND DEFEAT HIM IN HIS EFFORTS TO ENTICE ME TO BE **GREEDY**. THIS AFFIRMATION WILL NOW PENETRATE TO THE VERY DEPTHS OF MY MIND, BODY, AND SPIRIT IN THE SACRED NAME OF JESUS CHRIST, AMEN.

74. **GRUDGING** – HEAVENLY FATHER, WITH THE AID OF JESUS CHRIST AND THE HOLY GHOST,

AND WITH THEIR UNCONDITIONAL LOVE FOR ME AND ME FOR THEM, PLEASE BLESS ME WITH THE FAITH, COURAGE, ABILITY, DESIRE, AND THE WILLINGNESS TO LISTEN TO AND HEED THE PROMPTINGS OF THE HOLY GHOST IN PREFERENCE TO THOSE OF THE DEVIL AND HIS MINIONS IN THEIR EFFORTS TO ENTICE ME TO HARBOR **GRUDGES** AGAINST THOSE WHO HAVE OFFENDED ME IN SOME WAY. THIS AFFIRMATION WILL NOW PENETRATE TO THE VERY DEPTHS OF MY MIND, BODY, AND SPIRIT IN THE SACRED NAME OF JESUS CHRIST, AMEN.

75. ***HOSTILITY*** – HEAVENLY FATHER, WITH THE AID OF JESUS CHRIST AND THE HOLY GHOST, AND WITH THEIR UNCONDITIONAL LOVE FOR ME AND ME FOR THEM, PLEASE BLESS ME WITH THE ABILITY, DESIRE, FAITH, COURAGE, AND WILLINGNESS TO LISTEN TO AND HEED THE HOLY GHOST IN PREFERENCE TO THOSE OF THE DEVIL AND HIS MINIONS IN THEIR EFFORTS TO ENTICE ME TO BE **HOSTILE** TO OTHERS WHO HAVE OFFENDED ME AND OTHERS IN SOME WAY. THIS AFFIRMATION WILL NOW PENETRATE TO THE VERY DEPTHS OF MY MIND, BODY, AND SPIRIT IN THE SACRED NAME OF JESUS CHRIST, AMEN.

76. ***HATE*** – HEAVENLY FATHER, WITH THE AID OF JESUS CHRIST AND THE HOLY GHOST, AND WITH THEIR UNCONDITIONAL LOVE FOR ME AND ME FOR THEM, PLEASE BLESS ME WITH THE ABILITY, DESIRE, FAITH, COURAGE, AND THE WILLINGNESS TO LISTEN TO AND HEED THE PROMPTINGS OF THE HOLY GHOST IN PREFERENCE TO THE DEVIL AND HIS MINIONS

IN THEIR EFFORTS TO ENTICE ME TO **HATE** SOMEONE OR SOME ACTIVITY WHICH HAS OFFENDED ME IN SOME WAY. THIS AFFIRMATION WILL NOW PENETRATE TO THE VERY DEPTHS OF MY MIND, BODY, AND SPIRIT IN THE SACRED NAME OF JESUS CHRIST, AMEN.

77. ***IRREVERENCE*** – HEAVENLY FATHER, WITH THE AID OF JESUS CHRIST AND THE HOLY GHOST, AND WITH THEIR UNCONDITIONAL LOVE FOR ME AND ME FOR THEM, PLEASE BLESS ME WITH THE ABILITY, FAITH, COURAGE, DESIRE, AND THE WILLINGNESS TO LISTEN TO AND HEED THE PROMPTINGS OF THE HOLY GHOST AND IN PREFERENCE TO THOSE OF THE DEVIL AND HIS MINIONS IN THEIR EFFORTS TO INDUCE ME TO BE **IRREVERENT** TO THE DEITY AND OTHERS IN ALL SITUATIONS AND EVENTS. THIS AFFIRMATION WILL NOW PENETRATE TO THE VERY DEPTHS OF MY MIND, BODY, AND SPIRIT IN THE SACRED NAME OF JESUS CHRIST, AMEN.

78. ***JEALOUSY*** – HEAVENLY FATHER, WITH THE AID OF JESUS CHRIST AND THE HOLY GHOST, AND WITH THEIR UNCONDITIONAL LOVE FOR ME AND ME FOR THEM, PLEASE BLESS ME WITH THE ABILITY, DESIRE, FAITH, COURAGE, AND THE WILLINGNESS TO LISTEN TO AND HEED THE PROMPTINGS OF THE HOLY GHOST AND IN PREFERENCE TO THOSE OF THE DEVIL AND HIS MINIONS IN THEIR EFFORTS TO INDUCE ME TO BE **JEALOUS** OF OTHERS FOR WHAT THEY HAVE AND WHAT THEY ARE. THIS AFFIRMATION WILL NOW PENETRATE TO THE VERY DEPTHS OF MY MIND, BODY, AND SPIRIT IN THE SACRED NAME OF JESUS CHRIST, AMEN.

79. **_LYING_** – HEAVENLY FATHER, WITH THE AID OF JESUS CHRIST AND THE HOLY GHOST, AND WITH THEIR UNCONDITIONAL LOVE FOR ME AND ME FOR THEM, PLEASE BLESS ME WITH THE COURAGE, ABILITY, FAITH, DESIRE, AND THE WILLINGNESS TO LISTEN TO AND HEED THE PROMPTINGS OF THE HOLY GHOST AND IN PREFERENCE TO THOSE OF THE DEVIL AND HIS MINIONS IN THEIR EFFORTS TO INDUCE ME TO **LIE** ABOUT ANYTHING AND EVERYTHING. THIS AFFIRMATION WILL NOW PENETRATE TO THE VERY DEPTHS OF MY MIND, BODY, AND SPIRIT IN THE SACRED NAME OF JESUS CHRIST, AMEN.

80. **_MERCY_** – HEAVENLY FATHER, WITH THE AID OF JESUS CHRIST AND THE HOLY GHOST, AND WITH THEIR UNCONDITIONAL LOVE FOR ME AND ME FOR THEM, PLEASE BLESS ME WITH THE COURAGE, ABILITY, FAITH, DESIRE, AND THE WILLINGNESS TO LISTEN TO AND HEED THE PROMPTINGS OF THE HOLY GHOST AND IN PREFERENCE TO THOSE OF THE DEVIL AND HIS MINIONS IN THEIR EFFORTS TO INDUCE ME TO HAVE **NO MERCY** ON THOSE WHO OFFEND ME, MY FAMILY, FRIENDS, AND NEIGHBORS. THIS AFFIRMATION WILL NOW PENETRATE TO THE VERY DEPTHS OF MY MIND, BODY, AND SPIRIT IN THE SACRED NAME OF JESUS CHRIST, AMEN.

81. **_MALICE_** - HEAVENLY FATHER, WITH THE AID OF JESUS CHRIST AND THE HOLY GHOST, AND WITH THEIR UNCONDITIONAL LOVE FOR ME AND ME FOR THEM, PLEASE BLESS ME WITH THE ABILITY, FAITH, DESIRE, COURAGE, AND WILLINGNESS TO LISTEN TO AND HEED THE PROMPTINGS OF THE HOLY GHOST AND IN

PREFERENCE TO THOSE OF THE DEVIL AND HIS MINIONS IN THEIR EFFORTS TO GENERATE AND MAGNIFY **MALICE** TOWARDS THOSE WHO OFFEND ME AND OTHERS. THIS AFFIRMATION WILL NOW PENETRATE TO THE VERY DEPTHS OF MY MIND, BODY, AND SPIRIT IN THE SACRED NAME OF JESUS CHRIST, AMEN.

82. ***NON-REPENTANCE*** – HEAVENLY FATHER, WITH THE AID OF JESUS CHRIST AND THE HOLY GHOST, AND WITH THEIR UNCONDITIONAL LOVE FOR ME AND ME FOR THEM, PLEASE BLESS ME WITH THE ABILITY, FAITH, COURAGE, DESIRE, AND THE WILLINGNESS TO LISTEN TO AND HEED THE PROMPTINGS OF THE HOLY GHOST AND IN PREFERENCE TO THOSE OF THE DEVIL AND HIS MINIONS IN THEIR EFFORTS TO PREVENT ME FROM **REPENTING** OF MY SINS ON A DAILY BASIS. THIS AFFIRMATION WILL NOW PENETRATE TO THE VERY DEPTHS OF MY MIND, BODY, AND SPIRIT IN THE SACRED NAME OF JESUS CHRIST, AMEN.

83. ***PREJUDICE*** – HEAVENLY FATHER, WITH THE AID OF JESUS CHRIST AND THE HOLY GHOST, AND WITH THEIR UNCONDITIONAL LOVE FOR ME AND ME FOR THEM, PLEASE BLESS ME WITH THE ABILITY, FAITH, COURAGE, DESIRE, AND THE WILLINGNESS TO LISTEN TO AND HEED THE PROMPTINGS OF THE HOLY GHOST AND IN PREFERENCE TO THOSE OF THE DEVIL AND HIS MINIONS IN THEIR EFFORTS TO CREATE AND MAGNIFY **PREJUDICES AND BIASES** IN MY LIFE. THIS AFFIRMATION WILL NOW PENETRATE TO THE VERY DEPTHS OF MY MIND, BODY, AND SPIRIT IN THE SACRED NAME OF JESUS CHRIST, AMEN.

84. ***PRIDE*** – HEAVENLY FATHER, WITH THE AID OF JESUS CHRIST AND THE HOLY GHOST, AND WITH THEIR UNCONDITIONAL LOVE FOR ME AND ME FOR THEM, PLEASE BLESS ME WITH THE ABILITY, FAITH, COURAGE, DESIRE, AND THE WILLINGNESS TO LISTEN TO AND HEED THE PROMPTINGS OF THE HOLY GHOST AND IN PREFERENCE TO THOSE OF THE DEVIL AND HIS MINIONS IN THEIR EFFORTS TO CREATE AND MAGNIFY THE EVIL TRAIT OF **PRIDE** IN ALL MY DEALINGS WITH THOSE WHOM I COME IN CONTACT. THIS AFFIRMATION WILL NOW PENETRATE TO THE VERY DEPTHS OF MY MIND, BODY, AND SPIRIT IN THE SACRED NAME OF JESUS CHRIST, AMEN.

85. ***RESENTMENT*** – HEAVENLY FATHER, WITH THE AID OF JESUS CHRIST AND THE HOLY GHOST, AND WITH THEIR UNCONDITIONAL LOVE FOR ME AND ME FOR THEM, PLEASE BLESS ME WITH THE ABILITY, FAITH, COURAGE, DESIRE, AND WILLINGNESS TO LISTEN TO AND HEED THE PROMPTINGS OF THE HOLY GHOST AND IN PREFERENCE TO THOSE OF THE DEVIL AND HIS MINIONS IN THEIR EFFORTS TO CREATE AND AMPLIFY THE EVIL TRAIT OF **RESENTMENT** TOWARD ANY WHO OFFEND ME OR THOSE WITH WHOM I COME IN CONTACT. THIS AFFIRMATION WILL NOW PENETRATE TO THE VERY DEPTHS OF MY MIND, BODY, AND SPIRIT IN THE HOLY NAME OF JESUS CHRIST, AMEN.

86. ***REVENGE*** – HEAVENLY FATHER, WITH THE AID OF JESUS CHRIST AND THE HOLY GHOST, AND WITH THEIR UNCONDITIONAL LOVE FOR ME AND ME FOR THEM, PLEASE BLESS ME WITH

THE ABILITY, FAITH, COURAGE, DESIRE, AND THE WILLINGNESS TO LISTEN TO AND HEED THE PROMPTINGS OF THE HOLY GHOST AND IN PREFERENCE TO THOSE OF THE DEVIL AND HIS MINIONS IN THEIR EFFORTS TO CREATE AND MAGNIFY THE EVIL TRAIT OF **REVENGE** TO GET EVEN WITH THOSE WHO HAVE OFFENDED ME. THIS AFFIRMATION WILL NOW PENETRATE TO THE VERY DEPTHS OF MY MIND, BODY, AND SPIRIT IN THE HOLY NAME OF JESUS CHRIST, AMEN.

87. ***RIVALRY*** – HEAVENLY FATHER, WITH THE AID OF JESUS CHRIST AND THE HOLY GHOST, AND WITH THEIR UNCONDITIONAL LOVE FOR ME AND ME FOR THEM, PLEASE BLESS ME WITH THE ABILITY, FAITH, COURAGE, DESIRE, AND WILLINGNESS TO LISTEN TO AND HEED THE PROMPTINGS OF THE HOLY GHOST AND IN PREFERENCE TO THOSE OF THE DEVIL AND HIS MINION IN THEIR EFFORTS TO CREATE A **RIVALRY** IN MY ASSOCIATION WITH OTHERS. THIS AFFIRMATION WILL NOW PENETRATE TO THE VERY DEPTHS OF MY MIND, BODY, AND SPIRIT IN THE SACRED NAME OF JESUS CHRIST, AMEN.

88. ***SNOBBISHNESS*** – HEAVENLY FATHER, WITH THE AID OF JESUS CHRIST AND THE HOLY GHOST, AND WITH THEIR UNCONDITIONAL LOVE FOR ME AND ME FOR THEM, PLEASE BLESS ME WITH THE ABILITY, FAITH, COURAGE, DESIRE, AND WILLINGNESS TO LISTEN TO AND HEED THE PROMPTINGS OF THE HOLY GHOST AND IN PREFERENCE TO THOSE OF SATAN AND HIS MINIONS IN THEIR EFFORTS TO HAVE ME

BELIEVE THAT I AM **SNOBBISH** AND AM BETTER THAN OTHERS. THIS AFFIRMATION WILL NOW PENETRATE TO THE VERY DEPTHS OF MY MIND, BODY, AND SPIRIT IN THE SACRED NAME OF JESUS CHRIST, AMEN.

89. *UNCHASTE* – HEAVENLY FATHER, WITH THE AID OF JESUS CHRIST AND THE HOLY GHOST, AND WITH THEIR UNCONDITIONAL LOVE FOR ME AND ME FOR THEM, PLEASE BLESS ME WITH THE ABILITY, FAITH, COURAGE, DESIRE, AND THE WILLINGNESS TO LISTEN TO AND HEED THE PROMPTINGS OF THE HOLY GHOST AND IN PREFERENCE TO THOSE OF THE DEVIL AND HIS MINIONS IN THEIR EFFORTS TO TEMPT ME TO BE **UNCHASTE** AND VIOLATE MY COVENANTS WITH MY LORD AND SAVIOR. THIS AFFIRMATION WILL NOW PENETRATE TO THE VERY DEPTHS OF MY MIND, BODY, AND SPIRIT IN THE SACRED NAME OF JESUS CHRIST, AMEN.

90. *UNFORGIVING* – HEAVENLY FATHER, WITH THE AID OF JESUS CHRIST AND THE HOLY GHOST, AND WITH THEIR UNCONDITIONAL LOVE FOR ME AND ME FOR THEM, PLEASE BLESS ME WITH THE ABILITY, FAITH, COURAGE, DESIRE, AND WILLINGNESS TO LISTEN TO AND HEED THE PROMPTINGS OF THE HOLY GHOST AND IN PREFERENCE TO THOSE OF THE DEVIL AND HIS MINIONS IN THEIR EFFORTS TO HAVE ME BE **UNFORGIVING** OF THOSE WHO HAVE OFFENDED ME. THIS AFFIRMATION WILL NOW PENETRATE TO THE VERY DEPTHS OF MY MIND, BODY, AND SPIRIT IN THE HOLY NAME OF JESUS CHRIST, AMEN.

91. ***NON-PRAYERFUL*** – HEAVENLY FATHER, WITH THE AID OF JESUS CHRIST AND THE HOLY GHOST, AND WITH THEIR UNCONDITIONAL LOVE FOR ME AND ME FOR THEM, PLEASE BLESS ME WITH THE ABILITY, FAITH, COURAGE, DESIRE, AND THE WILLINGNESS TO LISTEN TO AND HEED THE PROMPTINGS OF THE HOLY GHOST, IN PREFERENCE TO THOSE OF THE DEVIL AND HIS MINIONS IN THEIR EFFORTS TO MAKE ME BELIEVE THAT **PRAYER** IS AN EFFORT IN FUTILITY OR THAT GOD WILL NOT LISTEN ANYWAY. THIS AFFIRMATION WILL NOW PENETRATE TO THE VERY DEPTHS OF MY MIND, BODY, AND SPIRIT IN THE SACRED NAME OF JESUS CHRIST, AMEN.

92. ***UNRIGHTEOUSNESS*** – HEAVENLY FATHER, WITH THE AID OF JESUS CHRIST AND THE HOLY GHOST, AND WITH THEIR UNCONDITIONAL LOVE FOR ME AND ME FOR THEM, PLEASE BLESS ME WITH THE ABILITY, FAITH, COURAGE, DESIRE, AND WILLINGNESS TO LISTEN TO AND HEED THE PROMPTINGS OF THE HOLY GHOST, IN PREFERENCE TO THOSE OF THE DEVIL AND HIS MINIONS IN THEIR EFFORTS TO HAVE ME LIVE AN **UNRIGHTEOUS** AND EVIL LIFE. THIS AFFIRMATION WILL NOW PENETRATE TO THE VERY DEPTHS OF MY MIND, BODY, AND SPIRIT IN THE SACRED NAME OF JESUS CHRIST, AMEN.

93. ***UNTEACHABLE*** – HEAVENLY FATHER, WITH THE AID OF JESUS CHRIST AND THE HOLY GHOST, AND WITH THEIR UNCONDITIONAL LOVE FOR ME AND ME FOR THEM, PLEASE BLESS ME WITH THE ABILITY, FAITH, COURAGE, DESIRE, AND THE WILLINGNESS TO LISTEN TO AND HEED

THE PROMPTINGS OF THE HOLY GHOST IN PREFERENCE TO THOSE OF THE DEVIL AND HIS MINIONS IN THEIR EFFORTS TO DISCOURAGE ME FROM READING, STUDYING THE GOSPEL, AND BEING **UNTEACHABLE** IN ALL RIGHTEOUS ENDEAVORS. THIS AFFIRMATION WILL NOW PENETRATE TO THE VERY DEPTHS OF MY BODY, MIND, AND SPIRIT IN THE SACRED NAME OF JESUS CHRIST, AMEN.

94. *UNTRUSTWORTHY* – HEAVENLY FATHER, WITH THE AID OF JESUS CHRIST AND THE HOLY GHOST, AND WITH THEIR UNCONDITIONAL LOVE FOR ME AND ME FOR THEM, PLEASE BLESS ME WITH THE ABILITY, FAITH, COURAGE, DESIRE, AND THE WILLINGNESS TO LISTEN TO AND HEED THE PROMPTINGS OF THE HOLY GHOST, IN PREFERENCE TO THOSE OF THE DEVIL AND HIS MINIONS IN THEIR EFFORTS TO ENCOURAGE ME TO BE **UNTRUSTWORTHY** IN ALL MY DEALINGS WITH MY FELLOWMAN. THIS AFFIRMATION WILL NOW PENETRATE TO THE VERY DEPTHS OF MY MIND, BODY, AND SPIRIT IN THE SACRED NAME OF JESUS CHRIST, AMEN.

95. *WEAKNESS* – HEAVENLY FATHER, WITH THE AID OF JESUS CHRIST AND THE HOLY GHOST, AND WITH THEIR UNCONDITIONAL LOVE FOR ME AND ME FOR THEM, PLEASE BLESS ME WITH THE ABILITY, FAITH, COURAGE, DESIRE, AND THE WILLINGNESS TO LISTEN TO AND HEED THE PROMPTINGS OF THE HOLY GHOST IN PREFERENCE TO THOSE OF THE DEVIL AND HIS MINIONS IN THEIR EFFORTS TO COMPEL ME TO EXPRESS **WEAKNESS** IN ALL OF MY DEALINGS

WITH MY FELLOWMAN. THIS AFFIRMATION WILL NOW PENETRATE TO THE VERY DEPTHS OF MY MIND, BODY, AND SPIRIT, IN THE SACRED NAME OF JESUS CHRIST, AMEN.

96. **NON-VIRTUOUS** – HEAVENLY FATHER, WITH THE AID OF JESUS CHRIST AND THE HOLY GHOST, AND WITH THEIR UNCONDITIONAL LOVE FOR ME AND ME FOR THEM, PLEASE BLESS ME WITH THE ABILITY, FAITH, COURAGE, DESIRE, AND THE WILLINGNESS TO LISTEN TO AND HEED THE PROMPTINGS OF THE HOLY GHOST, IN PREFERENCE TO THOSE OF THE DEVIL AND HIS MINIONS IN THEIR EFFORTS TO COMPEL ME TO BE **NON-VIRTUOUS** IN ALL OF MY DEALINGS WITH MY FELLOWMAN. THIS AFFIRMATION WILL NOW PENETRATE TO THE VERY DEPTHS OF MY MIND, BODY, AND SPIRIT IN THE SACRED NAME OF JESUS CHRIST, AMEN.

ANOTHER VERSION OF THE AFFIRMATIONS OF EVIL:

97. HEAVENLY FATHER, WITH THE AID OF JESUS CHRIST AND THE HOLY GHOST, AND WITH THEIR UNCONDITIONAL LOVE FOR ME AND ME FOR THEM, PLEASE HELP ME TO EXPUNGE AND ELIMINATE THE FOLLOWING EVIL, DESTRUCTIVE, TRAITS, AND CHARACTERISTICS FROM ALL OF MY THOUGHTS AND ACTIONS— **ANGER, APATHY,** AND **AVARICE**. I AM NOW EXTREMELY DETERMINED TO HONOR AND OBEY. THIS AFFIRMATION WILL PENETRATE TO THE VERY DEPTHS OF MY MIND, BODY, AND SPIRIT IN THE SACRED NAME OF JESUS CHRIST, AMEN.

98. HEAVENLY FATHER, WITH THE AID OF JESUS CHRIST AND THE HOLY GHOST, AND WITH THEIR UNCONDITIONAL LOVE FOR ME AND ME FOR THEM, PLEASE HELP ME EXPUNGE AND ELIMINATE THE FOLLOWING EVIL, DESTRUCTIVE TRAITS AND CHARACTERISTICS FROM ALL OF MY THOUGHTS AND ACTIONS— **BLINDNESS**, **CALLOUSNESS**, AND **CHEATING**. I AM NOW EXTREMELY DETERMINED TO HONOR AND OBEY THIS AFFIRMATION WHICH WILL PENETRATE TO THE VERY DEPTHS OF MY MIND, BODY, AND SPIRIT IN THE SACRED NAME OF JESUS CHRIST, AMEN.

99. HEAVENLY FATHER, WITH THE AID OF JESUS CHRIST AND THE HOLY GHOST, AND WITH THEIR UNCONDITIONAL LOVE FOR ME AND ME FOR THEM, PLEASE HELP ME EXPUNGE AND ELIMINATE THE FOLLOWING EVIL, DESTRUCTIVE TRAITS AND CHARACTERISTICS FROM ALL OF MY THOUGHTS AND ACTIONS— **CONTEMPT** AND **CONTENTION**. I AM NOW EXTREMELY DETERMINED TO HONOR AND OBEY THIS AFFIRMATION WHICH WILL PENETRATE TO THE VERY DEPTHS OF MY MIND, BODY, AND SPIRIT IN THE SACRED NAME OF JESUS CHRIST, AMEN.

100. HEAVENLY FATHER, WITH THE AID OF JESUS CHRIST AND THE HOLY GHOST, AND WITH THEIR UNCONDITIONAL LOVE FOR ME AND ME FOR THEM, PLEASE HELP ME EXPUNGE AND ELIMINATE THE FOLLOWING EVIL, DESTRUCTIVE TRAITS AND CHARACTERISTICS FROM ALL OF MY THOUGHTS AND ACTIONS— **COWARDICE**, **CRUELTY**, AND **DENIABILITY**.

I AM NOW EXTREMELY DETERMINED TO HONOR AND OBEY THIS AFFIRMATION WHICH WILL PENETRATE TO THE VERY DEPTHS OF MY MIND, BODY, AND SPIRIT IN THE SACRED NAME OF JESUS CHRIST, AMEN.

101. HEAVENLY FATHER, WITH THE AID OF JESUS CHRIST AND THE HOLY GHOST, AND WITH THEIR UNCONDITIONAL LOVE FOR ME AND ME FOR THEM, PLEASE HELP ME EXPUNGE AND ELIMINATE THE FOLLOWING EVIL, DESTRUCTIVE TRAITS AND CHARACTERISTICS FROM ALL OF MY THOUGHTS AND ACTIONS—**DEVILISHNESS**, **DISHONESTY**, AND **DISLOYALTY**. I AM NOW EXTREMELY DETERMINED TO HONOR AND OBEY THIS AFFIRMATION WHICH WILL PENETRATE TO THE VERY DEPTHS OF MY MIND, BODY, AND SPIRIT IN THE SACRED NAME OF JESUS CHRIST, AMEN.

102. HEAVENLY FATHER, WITH THE AID OF JESUS CHRIST AND THE HOLY GHOST, AND WITH THEIR UNCONDITIONAL LOVE FOR ME AND ME FOR THEM, PLEASE HELP ME EXPUNGE AND ELIMINATE THE FOLLOWING EVIL, DESTRUCTIVE TRAITS AND CHARACTERISTICS FROM ALL OF MY THOUGHTS AND ACTIONS—**DISDAIN**, **DESTRUCTION**, AND **DOUBT**. I AM NOW EXTREMELY DETERMINED TO HONOR AND OBEY THIS AFFIRMATION WHICH WILL PENETRATE TO THE VERY DEPTHS OF MY MIND, BODY, AND SPIRIT IN THE SACRED NAME OF JESUS CHRIST, AMEN.

103. HEAVENLY FATHER, WITH THE AID OF JESUS CHRIST AND THE HOLY GHOST, AND WITH THEIR UNCONDITIONAL LOVE FOR ME AND ME FOR THEM, PLEASE HELP ME EXPUNGE AND ELIMINATE THE FOLLOWING EVIL, DESTRUCTIVE TRAITS AND CHARACTERISTICS FROM ALL OF MY THOUGHTS AND ACTIONS—**DISOBEDIENCE**, **DISORDER**, AND **DISORGANIZATION**. I AM NOW EXTREMELY DETERMINED TO HONOR AND OBEY THIS AFFIRMATION, WHICH WILL PENETRATE TO THE VERY DEPTHS OF MY MIND, BODY, AND SPIRIT IN THE SACRED NAME OF JESUS CHRIST, AMEN.

104. HEAVENLY FATHER, WITH THE AID OF JESUS CHRIST AND THE HOLY GHOST, AND WITH THEIR UNCONDITIONAL LOVE FOR ME AND ME FOR THEM, PLEASE HELP ME EXPUNGE AND ELIMINATE THE FOLLOWING EVIL, DESTRUCTIVE TRAITS AND CHARACTERISTICS FROM ALL OF MY THOUGHTS AND ACTIONS—**DREAD**, **ENSLAVEMENT**, AND **ENVY**. I AM NOW EXTREMELY DETERMINED TO HONOR AND OBEY THIS AFFIRMATION WHICH WILL PENETRATE TO THE VERY DEPTHS OF MY MIND, BODY, AND SPIRIT IN THE SACRED NAME OF JESUS CHRIST, AMEN.

105. HEAVENLY FATHER, WITH THE AID OF JESUS CHRIST AND THE HOLY GHOST, AND WITH THEIR UNCONDITIONAL LOVE FOR ME AND ME FOR THEM, PLEASE HELP ME EXPUNGE AND ELIMINATE THE FOLLOWING EVIL, DESTRUCTIVE TRAITS AND CHARACTERISTICS FROM ALL OF MY THOUGHTS AND ACTIONS—

EVIL, GOSSIPING, AND **GREED.** I AM EXTREMELY DETERMINED TO HONOR AND OBEY THIS AFFIRMATION, WHICH WILL PENETRATE TO THE VERY DEPTHS OF MY MIND, BODY, AND SPIRIT IN THE SACRED NAME OF JESUS CHRIST AMEN.

106. HEAVENLY FATHER, WITH THE AID OF JESUS CHRIST AND THE HOLY GHOST, AND WITH THEIR UNCONDITIONAL LOVE FOR ME AND ME FOR THEM, PLEASE HELP ME EXPUNGE AND ELIMINATE THE FOLLOWING EVIL, DESTRUCTIVE TRAITS AND CHARACTERISTICS FROM ALL OF MY THOUGHTS AND ACTIONS— **HOSTILITY, HARD-HEARTEDNESS,** AND **HATE.** I AM EXTREMELY DETERMINED TO HONOR AND OBEY THIS AFFIRMATION WHICH WILL PENETRATE TO THE VERY DEPTHS OF MY MIND, BODY, AND SPIRIT IN THE SACRED NAME OF JESUS CHRIST, AMEN.

107. HEAVENLY FATHER, WITH THE AID OF JESUS CHRIST AND THE HOLY GHOST, AND WITH THEIR UNCONDITIONAL LOVE FOR ME AND ME FOR THEM, PLEASE HELP ME EXPUNGE AND ELIMINATE THE FOLLOWING EVIL, DESTRUCTIVE TRAITS AND CHARACTERISTICS FROM ALL OF MY THOUGHTS AND ACTIONS— **INTOLERANCE, IRREVERENCE,** AND **IRRESPONSIBILITY.** I AM EXTREMELY DETERMINED TO HONOR AND OBEY THIS AFFIRMATION, WHICH WILL PENETRATE TO THE VERY DEPTHS OF MY MIND, BODY, AND SPIRIT IN THE SACRED NAME OF JESUS CHRIST, AMEN.

108. HEAVENLY FATHER, WITH THE AID OF JESUS CHRIST AND THE HOLY GHOST, AND WITH THEIR UNCONDITIONAL LOVE FOR ME AND ME FOR THEM, PLEASE HELP ME TO EXPUNGE AND ELIMINATE THE FOLLOWING EVIL, DESTRUCTIVE TRAITS AND CHARACTERISTICS FROM ALL OF MY THOUGHTS AND ACTIONS—**INSINCERITY**, **JEALOUSY**, AND **LAZINESS**. I AM NOW EXTREMELY DETERMINED TO HONOR AND OBEY THIS AFFIRMATION WHICH WILL PENETRATE TO THE VERY DEPTHS OF MY MIND, BODY, AND SPIRIT IN THE SACRED NAME OF JESUS CHRIST, AMEN.

109. HEAVENLY FATHER, WITH THE AID OF JESUS CHRIST AND THE HOLY GHOST, AND WITH THEIR UNCONDITIONAL LOVE FOR ME AND ME FOR THEM, PLEASE HELP ME TO EXPUNGE AND ELIMINATE THE FOLLOWING EVIL, DESTRUCTIVE TRAITS AND CHARACTERISTICS FROM ALL OF MY THOUGHTS AND ACTIONS—**LYING**, **LUST**, AND **MALEVOLENCE**. I AM EXTREMELY DETERMINED TO HONOR AND OBEY THIS AFFIRMATION WHICH WILL PENETRATE TO THE VERY DEPTHS OF MY MIND, BODY, AND SPIRIT IN THE SACRED NAME OF JESUS CHRIST, AMEN.

110. HEAVENLY FATHER, WITH THE AID OF JESUS CHRIST AND THE HOLY GHOST, AND WITH THEIR UNCONDITIONAL LOVE FOR ME AND ME FOR THEM, PLEASE HELP ME TO EXPUNGE AND ELIMINATE THE FOLLOWING EVIL, DESTRUCTIVE TRAITS AND CHARACTERISTICS FROM ALL OF MY THOUGHTS AND ACTIONS—**MALICE**, **MEANNESS**, AND **MERCILESSNESS**.

I AM EXTREMELY DETERMINED TO HONOR AND OBEY THIS AFFIRMATION, WHICH WILL PENETRATE TO THE VERY DEPTHS OF MY MIND, BODY, AND SPIRIT IN THE SACRED NAME OF JESUS CHRIST, AMEN.

111. HEAVENLY FATHER, WITH THE AID OF JESUS CHRIST AND THE HOLY GHOST, AND WITH THEIR UNCONDITIONAL LOVE FOR ME AND ME FOR THEM, PLEASE HELP ME TO EXPUNGE AND ELIMINATE THE FOLLOWING EVIL, DESTRUCTIVE TRAITS AND CHARACTERISTICS FROM ALL OF MY THOUGHTS AND ACTIONS—**NEGATIVITY, NON-COMMITMENT**, AND **NON-CARING**. I AM EXTREMELY DETERMINED TO HONOR AND OBEY THIS AFFIRMATION, WHICH WILL PENETRATE TO THE VERY DEPTHS OF MY MIND, BODY, AND SPIRIT IN THE SACRED NAME OF JESUS CHRIST, AMEN.

112. HEAVENLY FATHER, WITH THE AID OF JESUS CHRIST AND THE HOLY GHOST, AND WITH THEIR UNCONDITIONAL LOVE FOR ME AND ME FOR THEM, PLEASE HELP ME TO EXPUNGE AND ELIMINATE THE FOLLOWING EVIL, DESTRUCTIVE TRAITS AND CHARACTERISTICS FROM ALL OF MY THOUGHTS AND ACTIONS—**NON-CREATIVITY, NON-DEDICATION**, AND **NON-DISCERNING**. I AM EXTREMELY DETERMINED TO HONOR AND OBEY THIS AFFIRMATION, WHICH WILL PENETRATE TO THE VERY DEPTHS OF MY MIND, BODY, AND SPIRIT IN THE SACRED NAME OF JESUS CHRIST, AMEN.

113. HEAVENLY FATHER, WITH THE AID OF JESUS CHRIST AND THE HOLY GHOST, AND WITH

THEIR UNCONDITIONAL LOVE FOR ME AND ME FOR THEM, PLEASE HELP ME TO EXPUNGE AND ELIMINATE THE FOLLOWING EVIL, DESTRUCTIVE TRAITS AND CHARACTERISTICS FROM ALL OF MY THOUGHTS AND ACTIONS—**UNEMPATHETIC**, **NON-DEPENDENT**, AND **UNDISCIPLINED**. I AM EXTREMELY DETERMINED TO HONOR AND OBEY THIS AFFIRMATION, WHICH WILL PENETRATE TO THE VERY DEPTHS OF MY MIND, BODY, AND SPIRIT IN THE SACRED NAME OF JESUS CHRIST, AMEN.

114. HEAVENLY FATHER, WITH THE AID OF JESUS CHRIST AND THE HOLY GHOST, AND WITH THEIR UNCONDITIONAL LOVE FOR ME AND ME FOR THEM, PLEASE HELP ME TO EXPUNGE AND ELIMINATE THE FOLLOWING EVIL, DESTRUCTIVE TRAITS AND CHARACTERISTICS FROM ALL OF MY THOUGHTS AND ACTIONS—**NON-MEDITATIVE**, **UNMOTIVATED**, AND **NON-PERSISTENT**. I AM EXTREMELY DETERMINED TO HONOR AND OBEY THIS AFFIRMATION WHICH WILL PENETRATE TO THE VERY DEPTHS OF MY MIND, BODY, AND SPIRIT IN THE SACRED NAME OF JESUS CHRIST, AMEN.

115. HEAVENLY FATHER, WITH THE AID OF JESUS CHRIST AND THE HOLY GHOST, AND WITH THEIR UNCONDITIONAL LOVE FOR ME AND ME FOR THEM, PLEASE HELP ME TO EXPUNGE AND ELIMINATE THE FOLLOWING EVIL, DESTRUCTIVE TRAITS AND CHARACTERISTICS FROM ALL OF MY THOUGHTS AND ACTIONS—**UNREPENTANCE**, **NON-SEEKING**, AND **POLLUTING**. I AM NOW EXTREMELY DETERMINED TO HONOR AND

OBEY THIS AFFIRMATION, WHICH WILL PENETRATE TO THE VERY DEPTHS OF MY MIND, BODY, AND SPIRIT IN THE SACRED NAME OF JESUS CHRIST, AMEN.

116. HEAVENLY FATHER, WITH THE AID OF JESUS CHRIST AND THE HOLY GHOST, AND WITH THEIR UNCONDITIONAL LOVE FOR ME AND ME FOR THEM, PLEASE HELP ME TO EXPUNGE AND ELIMINATE THE FOLLOWING EVIL, DESTRUCTIVE TRAITS AND CHARACTERISTICS FROM ALL OF MY THOUGHTS AND ACTIONS— **PREJUDICE**, **PRIDE**, AND **PROCRASTINATION**. I AM NOW EXTREMELY DETERMINED TO HONOR AND OBEY THIS AFFIRMATION, WHICH WILL PENETRATE TO THE VERY DEPTHS OF MY MIND, BODY, AND SPIRIT IN THE SACRED NAME OF JESUS CHRIST, AMEN.

117. HEAVENLY FATHER, WITH THE AID OF JESUS CHRIST AND THE HOLY GHOST, AND WITH THEIR UNCONDITIONAL LOVE FOR ME AND ME FOR THEM, PLEASE HELP ME TO EXPUNGE AND ELIMINATE THE FOLLOWING EVIL, DESTRUCTIVE TRAITS AND CHARACTERISTICS FROM ALL OF MY THOUGHTS AND ACTIONS— **REVENGE**, **SELFISHNESS**, AND **EGOTISM**. I AM NOW EXTREMELY DETERMINED TO HONOR AND OBEY THIS AFFIRMATION, WHICH WILL PENETRATE TO THE VERY DEPTHS OF MY MIND, BODY, AND SPIRIT IN THE SACRED NAME OF JESUS CHRIST, AMEN.

118. HEAVENLY FATHER, WITH THE AID OF JESUS CHRIST AND THE HOLY GHOST, AND WITH THEIR UNCONDITIONAL LOVE FOR ME AND

ME FOR THEM, PLEASE HELP ME TO EXPUNGE AND ELIMINATE THE FOLLOWING EVIL, DESTRUCTIVE TRAITS AND CHARACTERISTICS FROM ALL OF MY THOUGHTS AND ACTIONS—**SNOBBISHNESS**, **SLOTHFULNESS**, AND **STRIFE**. I AM NOW EXTREMELY DETERMINED TO HONOR AND OBEY THIS AFFIRMATION, WHICH WILL PENETRATE TO THE VERY DEPTHS OF MY MIND, BODY, AND SPIRIT IN THE SACRED NAME OF JESUS CHRIST, AMEN.

119. HEAVENLY FATHER, WITH THE AID OF JESUS CHRIST AND THE HOLY GHOST, AND WITH THEIR UNCONDITIONAL LOVE FOR ME AND ME FOR THEM, PLEASE HELP ME TO EXPUNGE AND ELIMINATE THE FOLLOWING EVIL, DESTRUCTIVE TRAITS AND CHARACTERISTICS FROM ALL OF MY THOUGHTS AND ACTIONS—**SURRENDERING TO EVIL**, **TACTLESS**, AND **THANKLESS**. I AM NOW EXTREMELY DETERMINED TO OBEY THIS AFFIRMATION, WHICH WILL PENETRATE TO THE VERY DEPTHS OF MY MIND, BODY, AND SPIRIT IN THE SACRED NAME OF JESUS CHRIST, AMEN.

120. HEAVENLY FATHER, WITH THE AID OF JESUS CHRIST AND THE HOLY GHOST, AND WITH THEIR UNCONDITIONAL LOVE FOR ME AND ME FOR THEM, PLEASE HELP ME TO EXPUNGE AND ELIMINATE THE FOLLOWING EVIL, DESTRUCTIVE TRAITS AND CHARACTERISTICS FROM ALL OF MY THOUGHTS AND ACTIONS—**THOUGHTLESSNESS**, **UNCHASTE**, AND **UNDISCIPLINED**. I AM NOW EXTREMELY DETERMINED TO OBEY THIS AFFIRMATION,

WHICH WILL PENETRATE TO THE VERY DEPTHS OF MY MIND, BODY, AND SPIRIT IN THE SACRED NAME OF JESUS CHRIST, AMEN.

121. FATHER IN HEAVEN, WITH THE AID OF JESUS CHRIST AND THE HOLY GHOST, AND WITH THEIR UNCONDITIONAL LOVE FOR ME AND ME FOR THEM, PLEASE HELP ME TO EXPUNGE AND ELIMINATE THE FOLLOWING EVIL, DESTRUCTIVE TRAITS AND CHARACTERISTICS FROM ALL OF MY THOUGHTS AND ACTIONS—**NON-ENDURING**, **UNFORGIVING**, AND **LAWLESSNESS**. I AM NOW EXTREMELY DETERMINED TO OBEY THIS AFFIRMATION WHICH WILL PENETRATE TO THE VERY DEPTHS OF MY MIND, BODY, AND SPIRIT IN THE SACRED NAME OF JESUS CHRIST, AMEN.

122. HEAVENLY FATHER, WITH THE AID OF JESUS CHRIST AND THE HOLY GHOST, AND WITH THEIR UNCONDITIONAL LOVE FOR ME AND ME FOR THEM, PLEASE HELP ME TO EXPUNGE AND ELIMINATE THE FOLLOWING EVIL, DESTRUCTIVE TRAITS AND CHARACTERISTICS FROM ALL OF MY THOUGHTS AND ACTIONS—**NON-PRAYERFULNESS**, **UNPREPAREDNESS**, AND **UNRIGHTEOUSNESS**. I AM NOW EXTREMELY DETERMINED TO OBEY THIS AFFIRMATION WHICH WILL PENETRATE TO THE VERY DEPTHS OF MY MIND, BODY, AND SPIRIT IN THE SACRED NAME OF JESUS CHRIST, AMEN.

123. HEAVENLY FATHER, WITH THE AID OF JESUS CHRIST AND THE HOLY GHOST, AND

WITH THEIR UNCONDITIONAL LOVE FOR THEM AND THEY FOR ME, PLEASE HELP ME TO EXPUNGE AND ELIMINATE THE FOLLOWING EVIL, DESTRUCTIVE TRAITS AND CHARACTERISTICS FROM ALL OF MY THOUGHTS AND ACTIONS—**UNSURE, UNTEACHABLE**, AND **UNTRUSTWORTHY**. I AM NOW EXTREMELY DETERMINED TO OBEY THIS AFFIRMATION WHICH WILL PENETRATE TO THE VERY DEPTHS OF MY MIND, BODY, AND SPIRIT IN THE SACRED NAME OF JESUS CHRIST, AMEN.

124. HEAVENLY FATHER, WITH THE AID OF JESUS CHRIST AND THE HOLY GHOST, AND WITH THEIR UNCONDITIONAL LOVE FOR ME AND ME FOR THEM, PLEASE HELP ME TO EXPUNGE AND ELIMINATE THE FOLLOWING EVIL, DESTRUCTIVE TRAITS AND CHARACTERISTICS FROM ALL OF MY THOUGHTS AND ACTIONS—**UNVIRTUOUS, VACILLATION**, AND **WEAKNESS**. I AM NOW EXTREMELY DETERMINED TO OBEY THIS AFFIRMATION WHICH WILL PENETRATE TO THE VERY DEPTHS OF MY MIND, BODY, AND SPIRIT IN THE SACRED NAME OF JESUS CHRIST, AMEN.

We have been told many times that we must forgive others of their trespasses, but I know of no one that has really shown us how to do it. Just saying it and really meaning it are two different things. I believe the following affirmations will help.

These affirmations, in my estimation, are some of the most effective weapons we have to counteract many of the weapons Satan uses against us.

The following forgiveness affirmations are perhaps, the most important of all affirmations. These affirmations are aimed at forgiving our parents, brothers, sisters, grandparents, in-laws, aunts, uncles, close friends, relatives, enemies, and anyone who has physically, emotionally, or mentally injured us. They are all on God's commandment that we must forgive one another, or he cannot forgive us. Our forgiveness extends especially to ourselves. If we can't forgive ourselves, how can we forgive anyone else? Forgiveness always begins at home and within our own minds!

To forgive people such as Hitler, Stalin, or other evil leaders and authorities of their trespasses against humanity is not for us to forgive—only God has that privilege and responsibility unless their trespasses have directly affected us specifically.

Satan would be happy for us to carry our unforgiveness around with us forever like stones in a tote bag.

Here are some of the many forgiveness traits that will help us draw closer to our heavenly Father:

125. HEAVENLY FATHER, WITH THE AID OF JESUS CHRIST AND THE HOLY GHOST, AND WITH THEIR UNCONDITIONAL LOVE FOR ME AND ME FOR THEM, PLEASE BLESS ME WITH THE COURAGE, DESIRE, FAITH, WILLINGNESS, AND DETERMINATION TO FORGIVE MYSELF OF THE MANY UNREPENTANT SINS I HAVE COMMITTED AND THE IMPERFECTIONS I HAVE ACCUMULATED THROUGHOUT MY LIFE. I AM NOW EXTREMELY DETERMINED AND COMMITTED TO OBEYING THIS AFFIRMATION, WHICH WILL NOW PENETRATE TO THE VERY DEPTHS OF MY MIND, BODY, AND SPIRIT IN THE SACRED NAME OF JESUS CHRIST, AMEN.

126. HEAVENLY FATHER, WITH THE AID OF JESUS CHRIST AND THE HOLY GHOST, AND WITH THEIR UNCONDITIONAL LOVE FOR ME AND ME FOR THEM, PLEASE BLESS ME WITH THE FAITH, COURAGE, WILLINGNESS,

AND DETERMINATION TO GLADLY FORGIVE MY MOTHER FOR ALL OF THE TIMES SHE PUNISHED ME BOTH PHYSICALLY, MENTALLY, AND EMOTIONALLY. I AM NOW EXTREMELY DETERMINED AND COMMITTED TO OBEYING THIS AFFIRMATION, WHICH WILL PENETRATE TO THE VERY DEPTHS OF MY MIND, BODY, AND SPIRIT IN THE SACRED NAME OF JESUS CHRIST, AMEN.

127. HEAVENLY FATHER, WITH THE AID OF JESUS CHRIST AND THE HOLY GHOST, AND WITH THEIR UNCONDITIONAL LOVE FOR ME AND ME FOR THEM, PLEASE BLESS ME WITH THE COURAGE, FAITH, DESIRE, WILLINGNESS, AND DETERMINATION TO GLADLY FORGIVE MY FATHER FOR ALL OF THE TIMES HE OFFENDED ME BOTH PHYSICALLY, MENTALLY, AND EMOTIONALLY. I AM NOW EXTREMELY DETERMINED AND COMMITTED TO OBEY THIS AFFIRMATION WHICH WILL PENETRATE TO THE VERY DEPTHS OF MY MIND, BODY, AND SPIRIT IN THE SACRED NAME OF JESUS CHRIST, AMEN.

128. HEAVENLY FATHER, WITH THE AID OF JESUS CHRIST AND THE HOLY GHOST, AND WITH THEIR UNCONDITIONAL LOVE FOR ME AND ME FOR THEM, PLEASE BLESS ME WITH THE COURAGE, FAITH, DESIRE, WILLINGNESS, AND DETERMINATION TO GLADLY FORGIVE MY BROTHERS FOR ALL OF THE HARM AND PAIN THEY HAVE BOUGHT INTO MY LIFE PHYSICALLY, MENTALLY, AND EMOTIONALLY. I AM NOW EXTREMELY DETERMINED AND COMMITTED TO OBEY THIS AFFIRMATION

WHICH WILL PENETRATE TO THE VERY DEPTHS OF MY MIND, BODY, AND SPIRIT IN THE SACRED NAME OF JESUS CHRIST, AMEN.

129. HEAVENLY FATHER, WITH THE AID OF JESUS CHRIST AND THE HOLY GHOST, AND WITH THEIR UNCONDITIONAL LOVE FOR ME AND ME FOR THEM, PLEASE BLESS ME WITH THE COURAGE, FAITH, DESIRE, WILLINGNESS, AND DETERMINATION TO GLADLY FORGIVE MY SISTERS FOR ALL OF THE HARM AND PAIN THEY HAVE BROUGHT INTO MY LIFE PHYSICALLY, MENTALLY, AND EMOTIONALLY. I AM NOW EXTREMELY DETERMINED AND COMMITTED TO OBEY THIS AFFIRMATION WHICH WILL PENETRATE TO THE VERY DEPTHS OF MY MIND, BODY, AND SPIRIT IN THE SACRED NAME OF JESUS CHRIST, AMEN.

130. HEAVENLY FATHER, WITH THE AID OF JESUS CHRIST AND THE HOLY GHOST, AND WITH THEIR UNCONDITIONAL LOVE FOR ME AND ME FOR THEM, PLEASE BLESS ME WITH THE COURAGE, FAITH, ABILITY, DESIRE, WILLINGNESS, AND DETERMINATION TO GLADLY FORGIVE MY UNCLES FOR ALL OF THE HARM AND PAIN THEY HAVE BROUGHT INTO MY LIFE PHYSICALLY, MENTALLY, AND EMOTIONALLY. I AM NOW EXTREMELY DETERMINED AND COMMITTED TO OBEYING THIS AFFIRMATION, WHICH WILL PENETRATE TO THE VERY DEPTHS OF MY MIND, BODY, AND SPIRIT IN THE SACRED NAME OF JESUS CHRIST, AMEN.

131. HEAVENLY FATHER, WITH THE AID OF JESUS CHRIST AND THE HOLY GHOST, AND WITH THEIR UNCONDITIONAL LOVE FOR ME AND ME FOR THEM, PLEASE BLESS ME WITH THE COURAGE, FAITH, DESIRE, ABILITY, WILLINGNESS, AND DETERMINATION TO GLADLY FORGIVE MY AUNTS FOR ALL OF THE HARM AND PAIN THEY HAVE BROUGHT INTO MY LIFE PHYSICALLY, MENTALLY, AND EMOTIONALLY. I AM NOW EXTREMELY DETERMINED AND COMMITTED TO OBEY THIS AFFIRMATION WHICH WILL PENETRATE TO THE VERY DEPTHS OF MY MIND, BODY, AND SPIRIT IN THE SACRED NAME OF JESUS CHRIST, AMEN.

132. HEAVENLY FATHER, WITH THE AID OF JESUS CHRIST AND THE HOLY GHOST, AND WITH THEIR UNCONDITIONAL LOVE FOR ME AND ME FOR THEM, PLEASE BLESS ME WITH THE COURAGE, FAITH, DESIRE, ABILITY, WILLINGNESS, AND DETERMINATION TO GLADLY FORGIVE MY COUSINS FOR ALL OF THE PAIN THEY HAVE BROUGHT INTO MY LIFE PHYSICALLY, MENTALLY, AND EMOTIONALLY. I AM NOW EXTREMELY DETERMINED AND COMMITTED TO OBEY THIS AFFIRMATION WHICH WILL PENETRATE TO THE VERY DEPTHS OF MY MIND, BODY, AND SPIRIT IN THE SACRED NAME OF JESUS CHRIST, AMEN.

133. HEAVENLY FATHER, WITH THE AID OF JESUS CHRIST AND THE HOLY GHOST, AND WITH THEIR UNCONDITIONAL LOVE FOR ME AND ME FOR THEM, PLEASE BLESS ME WITH THE COURAGE, FAITH, DESIRE, ABILITY,

WILLINGNESS, AND DETERMINATION TO GLADLY FORGIVE EVERYONE ELSE THAT HAS BROUGHT ANY PAIN OR DISCOMFORT INTO MY LIFE PHYSICALLY, MENTALLY, AND EMOTIONALLY. I AM NOW EXTREMELY DETERMINED AND COMMITTED TO OBEY THIS AFFIRMATION WHICH WILL PENETRATE TO THE VERY DEPTHS OF MY MIND, BODY, AND SPIRIT IN THE SACRED NAME OF JESUS CHRIST, AMEN.

134. HEAVENLY FATHER, WITH THE AID OF JESUS CHRIST AND THE HOLY GHOST, AND WITH THEIR UNCONDITIONAL LOVE FOR ME AND ME FOR THEM, PLEASE HELP ME TO HAVE THE COURAGE, FAITH, DESIRE, ABILITY, WILLINGNESS, AND DETERMINATION TO EXPUNGE AND ELIMINATE THE FEAR AND ANXIETY ASSOCIATED WITH MY PAST UNREPENTANT INDISCRETIONS AND FOLLIES FOR WHICH I NOW ASK THEE FOR FORGIVENESS. I AM NOW EXTREMELY COMMITTED TO OBEY THIS AFFIRMATION WHICH WILL PENETRATE TO THE VERY DEPTHS OF MY BODY, MIND, AND SPIRIT IN THE SACRED NAME OF JESUS CHRIST, AMEN.

135. HEAVENLY FATHER, WITH THE AID OF JESUS CHRIST AND THE HOLY GHOST, AND WITH THEIR UNCONDITIONAL LOVE FOR ME AND ME FOR THEM, PLEASE BLESS ME WITH THE COURAGE, FAITH, DESIRE, ABILITY, WILLINGNESS, AND DETERMINATION TO EXPUNGE AND ELIMINATE THE RESENTMENT AND PROCRASTINATION ASSOCIATED WITH MY PAST INDISCRETIONS AND FOLLIES FOR

WHICH I NOW ASK THEE TO FORGIVE ME. I AM NOW EXTREMELY COMMITTED TO OBEYING THIS AFFIRMATION, WHICH WILL PENETRATE TO THE VERY DEPTHS OF MY MIND, BODY, AND SPIRIT IN THE SACRED NAME OF JESUS CHRIST, AMEN.

136. HEAVENLY FATHER, WITH THE AID OF JESUS CHRIST AND THE HOLY GHOST, AND WITH THEIR UNCONDITIONAL LOVE FOR ME AND ME FOR THEM, PLEASE BLESS ME WITH THE COURAGE, FAITH, DESIRE, WILLINGNESS, AND DETERMINATION TO EXPUNGE AND ELIMINATE THE ANGUISH AND GUILT ASSOCIATED WITH MY PAST INDISCRETIONS AND FOLLIES FOR WHICH I NOW ASK THEE TO FORGIVE ME. I AM NOW EXTREMELY COMMITTED TO OBEY THIS AFFIRMATION WHICH WILL PENETRATE TO THE VERY DEPTHS OF MY MIND, BODY, AND SPIRIT IN THE SACRED NAME OF JESUS CHRIST, AMEN.

137. HEAVENLY FATHER, WITH THE AID OF JESUS CHRIST AND THE HOLY GHOST, AND WITH THEIR UNCONDITIONAL LOVE FOR ME AND ME FOR THEM, PLEASE BLESS ME WITH THE COURAGE, FAITH, DESIRE, ABILITY, WILLINGNESS, AND DETERMINATION TO EXPUNGE AND ELIMINATE THE GRUDGES AND NON-FORGIVENESS ASSOCIATED WITH MY PAST INDISCRETIONS AND FOLLIES FOR WHICH I NOW ASK THEE TO FORGIVE ME. I AM NOW EXTREMELY COMMITTED TO OBEY THIS AFFIRMATION WHICH WILL PENETRATE TO THE VERY DEPTHS OF MY MIND, BODY, AND SPIRIT IN THE SACRED NAME OF JESUS CHRIST, AMEN.

138. HEAVENLY FATHER, WITH THE AID OF JESUS CHRIST AND THE HOLY GHOST, AND WITH THEIR UNCONDITIONAL LOVE FOR ME AND ME FOR THEM, PLEASE HELP ME TO HAVE THE COURAGE, FAITH, DESIRE, ABILITY, WILLINGNESS, AND DETERMINATION TO ACTIVATE MY FAITH TO ADOPT, MAGNIFY, AND EXPAND MY ABILITY TO RELEASE AND EXPUNGE **ALL BELIEFS, BELIEF SYSTEMS, AND TRADITIONS THAT LIMIT MY ABILITIES TO EXPAND AND OPEN MY MIND TO GREATER POSSIBILITIES FOR SPIRITUAL GROWTH, AND THE ABILITY TO DEFLECT SATAN'S TEMPTATIONS.** I NOW ASK THEE TO PLEASE FORGIVE ME FOR THESE SINS, FOLLY, AND INDISCRETIONS. I AM NOW EXTREMELY DETERMINED TO HONOR AND OBEY THIS AFFIRMATION WHICH WILL PENETRATE TO THE VERY DEPTHS OF MY MIND, BODY, AND SPIRIT IN THE SACRED NAME OF JESUS CHRIST, AMEN.

THE WAY TO WIN THIS WAR WITH SATAN IS FIRST: TO ACKNOWLEDGE THAT, INDEED, THERE IS A WAR GOING ON FOR THE SOULS OF MANKIND; SECOND: WE MUST BE DETERMINED AND WILLING TO JOIN FORCES WITH THE RIGHTEOUS WHO WILL ULTIMATELY WIN; THIRD: RECOGNIZE THAT THERE IS A NEEDED OPPOSITION IN ALL THINGS FOR US TO GROW SPIRITUALLY, SO WE MAY LIVE WITH THE HEAVENLY FATHER AGAIN AND THAT SATAN AND HIS MINIONS FILL THIS ROLE; FOURTH: THIS SCENARIO IS ESSENTIAL FOR THE SEPARATION OF THE WHEAT FROM THE TARES; AND FIFTH: WE MUST LOVE GOD, HIS SON JESUS CHRIST, AND THE HOLY GHOST UNCONDITIONALLY AND WITHOUT RESERVATION. THIS MEANS WE DO

NOT QUESTION HIS ACTIONS NOR METHODS BECAUSE WE ARE NOT QUALIFIED TO QUESTION. THE DEITY'S KNOWLEDGE, WISDOM, INTELLIGENCE, POWER, AND GLORY ARE SO FAR ABOVE OURS THAT IF EXPLAINED TO US, WE COULD NOT UNDERSTAND OR GRASP IT ALL. GOD HAS HIS REASONS FOR EVERYTHING HE DOES OR DOESN'T DO, AND IT IS ALL BECAUSE OF HIS GREAT LOVE FOR EVERY ONE OF US.

This may alleviate some of our questions, but the gist of this essay is to awaken the human family to the dangers of this war and use every means at their disposal to not only identify but also join the forces of righteousness and use the firepower that has been discussed in this work—all the scriptures—and use any other weapon that will counter the devastation and chaos generated by Satan and his forces.

Last of all, I wish to quote the book of Mormon from 1st. Nephi 12, verses 19 through 23:

> V 19 And while the angel spake these words, I beheld and saw that the seed of my brethren did contend against my seed, according to the word of the angel; and because of the pride of my seed, and the temptations of the devil, I beheld that the seed of my brethren did over-power the people of my seed.
>
> V 20 And it came to pass that I beheld and saw the people of the seed of my brethren that they had overcome my seed; and they went forth in multitudes upon the face of the land.
>
> V 21 And I saw them gathered together in multitudes; and I saw wars and rumors of wars among them; and in wars and rumors of wars I saw many generations pass away.
>
> V 22 And the angel said unto me: behold these shall dwindle in unbelief.
>
> V 23 And it came to pass that I beheld, after they had dwindled in unbelief they became a dark, and loathsome, and a filthy people, full of idleness and all manner of abominations.

In these verses, it is shown that the temptations of Satan caused the wars in which Nephi saw the extinction of his people and attributed it to the forces of evil. We should never underestimate the powers of Satan which we so readily succumb to and which brings about our downfall. The only power on earth that offsets Satan's power is the power of almighty God whom we should always heed. It is the only way we can get back into his presence.

CHAPTER FIFTEEN

Prayer and Supplication

Prayer, supplication, and meditation are among the greatest powers on earth as weapons against the satanic forces used against us. The act of prayer is an indication of our faith in the Deity, an acknowledgment of the existence of God and Jesus Christ in whose name we perform all activities related to righteousness in our physical world, and to the gospel of salvation. The more we learn to pray with true sincerity and faith, the more our prayers are likely to be answered. Prayer is so important in our fight against Lucifer and his minions that many of our prophets have admonished us to pray continually—pray every morning, every noon, and every night—pray for health, herds, crops, wisdom, knowledge, and understanding.

Those of us who do pray have our special times and places to approach God. My wife, Geri, besides family prayer, prays when she does the dishes, paints, or does other repetitious chores that require little concentration. For her, this seems to be the best time to pray and to receive answers as well. My greatest success occurs when I'm out driving or walking alone. During these periods, I can meditate without interruption and like Geri, I receive the answers to many questions and problems while so doing.

Another good time for prayer is during the Sacrament Ordinance. Several years ago, one of our prophets informed us that we could get closer to God during this period than at any other time excluding the Temple, both of which are good times and places to come 'clean' before God—ask his forgiveness and for the indiscretions inflicted on us by Satan. It is also an excellent time for deep reflection and meditation. These should be periods for self-analysis, goal setting, and making decisions in which areas of our lives need the most improvement. The Temple and Sacrament ordinances are quiet, sacred times that should be enjoyed and spent in communion with our Father in heaven.

Many people, including me, do not pray often enough nor with enough emotion, sincerity, and desire. Our prophets and church leaders spend a great amount of time on their knees and encourage us to do the same. Few of us spend the time on our knees as did Enos in the *Book of Mormon* who prayed mightily all day long and on into the night to gain a confirmation of the remission of his sins and attain a positive knowledge of God's forgiveness (Enos 1: 4-5). It would be advantageous to us all if we would develop this kind of determination, commitment, and faith.

Whether or not our prayers are answered depends on several things. Firstly, our Father in heaven treats us very much like we treat our own children when favors are requested. Many of us tend to withhold the requested item until it is earned. This is as it should be because God does the same with us. When repentant and obedient, we probably deserve what we have desired in our prayers. Then, if our faith is sufficient; if our prayers are sincere and from the heart; if the request is righteous and needful for ourselves and others, God may grant it. God knows what is best for us all, so not everything we request is freely given. Consequently, he may say 'no' even when we are worthy of receiving a sought-after blessing. This can either build or destroy our faith, depending on our attitude. If we recognize that God knows what is best for us and if he withholds a blessing, we can accept his decision in good faith. It is when we continually pester him that we may just get the thing for which we prayed, even though God knows it isn't in our best interest. We then must go through the painful process of learning by experience. After the trial is over, we may not be in such a hurry to pester him again when he has said no.

An example of a person pursuing a request after God has said no was that of prophet Joseph Smith and Martin Harris, where parts of the Book of Mormon were lost. Joseph, at Martin's insistence, kept asking for the transcript so he could show it to his wife. He was told no several times. Finally, to teach Joseph and all of us a lesson, God relented, and allowed the transcript to be taken, only to have it lost to the world. The lesson learned is to stop asking when God has said no!

Other important considerations that affect answers to our prayers are vain repetitions, emotional states, attitudes, love, and the intensity of our desires and enthusiasm. On the negative or destructive side of having our prayers answered are anger, hate, greed, moods, contention, deceit, disobedience, faithlessness, and pride. These are some of the many traits and characteristics that influence the answers to our prayers.

Vain repetitions deserve clarification. Webster's New World Dictionary gives the following definition of vanity: 1.) having no real value or significance, worthless, empty, idle, hollow, etc.; 2.) without force or effect, futile, fruitless, unprofitable, unavailing, etc.; 3.) having or showing excessively high regard for one's self, looks, possessions, abilities, etc. and indulging in or resulting from personal vanity, conceited; 4.) archaic, lacking in sense, foolish.

From this definition, we can understand why our Savior dislikes vain repetitions. It is an enemy to humility. If our prayers are idle, hollow, empty, and have no force, I believe God will not look upon them with any degree of interest. If we approach him under the influence of any of the counterproductive traits, it is unlikely that he will heed us. I'm sure that if repetitions are always sincere and are needed, God will heed our requests. The Lord's prayer is an example of repetition that if said in sincerity, will be answered.

My opinion is that our prayers will be answered if destructive traits such as anger, hate, greed, contempt, contention, doubt, hostility, irreverence, etc. are absent. God has given us the Lord's prayer as an example, but to repeat it day after day with no feeling, determination, or commitment, would be vain. To repeat it with feeling, commitment, and faith, I'm sure, would be much more acceptable to him. To repeat our own prayers with feeling, hope, and faith would probably be agreeable to him if the subject was righteous and included others in need.

Experience has shown that we are more apt to gain solace and comfort and receive answers to our prayers when we are in the depths of despair or when some crisis exists; when our emotions are deep and sincere and our concern for others is at a peak; and if we and those for whom we pray, deserve it. God is then much more likely to respond to our sincere supplications. He wants to help us and will if we learn to approach him in true humility. Seldom will we receive his help when we feel unworthy, unrepentant, or undeserving unless we are seeking his guidance to return to his presence.

The first step in making us worthy is sincere daily prayers and repentance. Our supplications must be with true honest feeling and emotion, never faked. We should also be hopeful, have faith, and pray only for that which is necessary for our sustenance, health, and other's ailments and what is needful for ours and others' salvation and survival. God will hear our prayers and give us the challenges we need for growth and spiritual progress. He always knows what is best for us but wants us to ask for it. It not only increases our faith but also helps us realize just how much we must depend on him for every needful thing.

The traits of humility, meekness, expectation, faith, and hope are among the more important attitudes we must demonstrate when approaching God in prayer. These traits when developed to their fullest are among the most effective weapons we can use against Satan and his minions. The realization that God is involved in every aspect of our lives is essential when we kneel before him. When we approach God in prayer and feel worthy of his blessings and that we deserve his help, he will give us the help if it is righteous and if he knows it will benefit us. Then, we will probably get that for which we pray.

Praying for God's help in overcoming Satan's temptations is probably the most vital thing we can do to oppose the powers of darkness, also asking for a remission of our sins and transgressions which puts us in a good position for the help we need to thwart the intrusion of Satan into our lives.

The trait and characteristic of love and its development are perhaps, the most important of all attributes we have available as a weapon to overcome the powers of evil.

A sample of unifying love attributes are listed here, keeping in mind that there are about 500 of them that need to be perfected before we can live with God and Jesus Christ in the Celestial kingdom. Nothing or no one that is unclean or imperfect can enter the kingdom of God [my opinion]. They are as follows:

Achievement, Appreciation, Affection, Beauty, Benevolence, Caring, Challenging, Changing, Charity, Chastity, Cleanliness, Commitment, Compassion, Confidence, Consideration, Consistency, Courage, Creativity, Dedication, Dignity, Diligence, Discernment, Empathy, Encouragement, Expectation, Faith, Forgiveness, Friendliness, Gentleness, Giving, Gratitude, Helpfulness, Honesty, Honor, Hopefulness, Humility, Insight, Innocence, Integrity, Intelligence, Justice, Kindness, Knowledge, Love, Loyalty, Mercy, Meekness, Modesty, Morality, Obedience, Obsequiousness, Oneness, Openness, Patience, Perseverance, Persistence, Prayerfulness, Preparedness, Promptness, Purity, Remorse, Repentance, Respectfulness, Responsibility, Reverence, Righteousness, Sacrifice, Self-Discipline, Self-Reliance, Sensitivity, Spirituality, Stability, Strength, Studiousness, Success-Oriented, Searching, Self-Control, Self-Esteem, Sympathy, Tactfulness, Temperance, Tenderness, Thoughtfulness, Thrift, Tolerance, Trustworthiness, Trusting, Understanding, Virtue, Wisdom, and Warmth.

The magnitude of God's love for us is mostly incomprehensible. It is difficult for us mortals to understand how he is able to love us all equally even when we are disobedient and rebellious. To develop and elevate our love to the same level as God's love for us, especially when we have great evils perpetrated against us, is far beyond our comprehension. It is easy to love those who are sweet, kind, and loving. The true test comes when we are required to love our enemies. Here we must rely on God's power, wisdom, knowledge, and intelligence to help us, first, to create the desire, then take the necessary actions to help us love them. This is only possible if we continue to express and increase our love for others. We cannot hoard our love and expect it to grow. We must develop and let it mature, give and accept it freely from others, and our prayers will take on a new meaning and be more acceptable to God. The growth of love and charity is absolutely necessary if we expect to reside with him again.

It is my opinion that the following are a few of the traits, attributes, and characteristics we must expunge and purge before we can live with God, Jesus Christ, and the Holy Ghost:

Anger, Apathy, Arrogance, Avarice, Bias, Blindness, Callousness, Cheating, Contempt, Contention, Controlling, Cowardly, Cruelty, deplorable, Despotic, Devilish, Discouragement, Dishonest, Disloyal, Disobedient, Disorderly, Disdainful, Destructive, Devilish, Doubting, Dreadful, Despicable, Envying, Evil-Minded, Faithless, Gossiping, Greedy, Hostile, Hardhearted, Hateful, Horrible, Insolent, Inebriation, Irreverent, Irresponsible, Insincere, Jealous, Lazy, Loveless, Lying, Lustful, Malevolent, Malicious, Manipulative, Mean, Merciless, Murderous, Negative, Uncommitted, Uncaring, Non-Creative, Non-Discerning, Non-Empathetic, Non-Dependent, Undisciplined, Non-Meditative, Non-Motivated, Non-Persistent, Non-Repentant, Non-Seeking, Obsession, Opinionated, Obnoxious, Obstinate, Odious, Offensive, Oppressive, Orneriness, Polluting, Prejudiced, Prideful, Procrastinating, Selfish, Self-Centered, Self-Satisfied Revengeful, Sadistic, Scornful, Sloppy, Seething, Smearing, Slothful, Spiteful, Sporadic, Superficial, Tactless, Terrible, Thankless, Thoughtless, Unchaste, Non-Enduring, Unforgiving, Unlawful, Non-Prayerful, Unprepared, Unrighteous, Unsure, Untrustworthy, Non-Virtuous, Vacillating, Vindictive, Vicious, Vitriol, and Weak-Minded.

These are a few of the approximately 500 destructive traits that must be eradicated from our vocal, mental, and physical activities. Remember that those unclean and imperfect humans cannot enter God's Celestial kingdom.

There are so many evils that I have not discussed that Satan and his destructive minions use every day on each and every one of us mortals that it would take volumes to discuss them all. I hope that I have created a desire in each of us to look at every aspect of our lives and the lives of others to determine the extent of Satan's involvement in our destruction. God will protect us from this destruction if we just pray for his help and act on his inspiration, guidance, and revelation which will completely offset the powers of the evil forces around us.

Knowing the extent of the powers of evil should create within us the desire to look within ourselves and adopt the path that God has set forth for us to follow, which leads to the perfection required to attain the Celestial kingdom where God dwells.

In summary, this work is intended to expose many of the lies, deceits, etc. In fact, it exposes what Satan and his followers are attempting to do to the human race spiritually, mentally, emotionally, and physically by destroying the love we have for each other and ourselves **THROUGH ACCUSATIONS AND EVERY OTHER METHOD THAT WORKS FOR HIM.**

I believe that without God's love, we would have nothing left but hate, fear, and all of the other destructive traits and characteristics to overcome which we cannot do alone without the help of God and his plan of salvation and exaltation.

If we acknowledge that Satan's influences and promptings on mankind are the perpetrators of the world's many problems and atrocities, we could then see the direction of his weapons' thrusts and take the necessary evasive actions.

Our major weapon is the willingness and determination to accept the love we have for and from the Deity and each other.

MAY GOD BLESS ALL OF OUR EFFORTS IN OUR STRUGGLE TO ATTAIN RESIDENCE WITH HIM, THROUGHOUT THE ETERNITIES!

www.ingramcontent.com/pod-product-compliance
Lightning Source LLC
Chambersburg PA
CBHW021446070526
44577CB00002B/281